HOT ROD

ROBERT E. PETERSEN AND THE CREATION OF THE WORLD'S MOST POPULAR CAR AND MOTORCYCLE MAGAZINES

EMPIRE

MATT STONE with GIGI CARLETON

FOREWORD BY
ED ISKENDERIAN

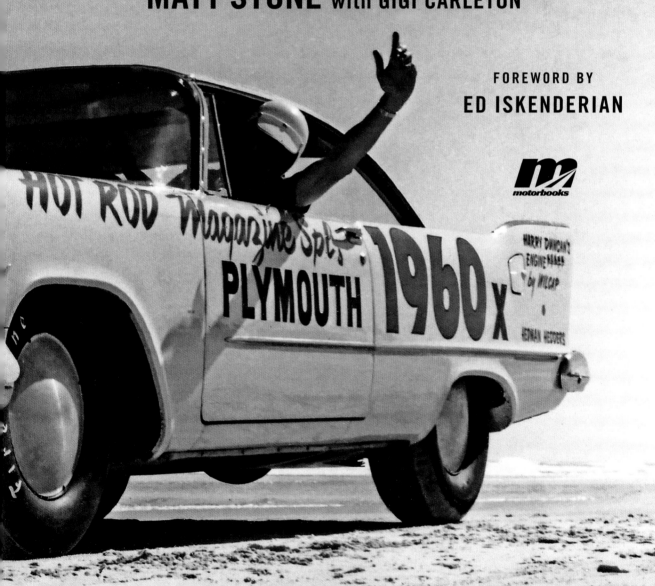

Brimming with creative inspiration, how-to projects, and useful information to enrich your everyday life, Quarto Knows is a favorite destination for those pursuing their interests and passions. Visit our site and dig deeper with our books into your area of interest: Quarto Creates, Quarto Cooks, Quarto Homes, Quarto Lives, Quarto Drives, Quarto Explores, Quarto Gifts, or Quarto Kids.

Inspiring | Educating | Creating | Entertaining

First published in 2018 by Motorbooks, an imprint of The Quarto Group, 401 Second Avenue North, Suite 310, Minneapolis, MN 55401 USA. T (612) 344-8100 F (612) 344-8692

www.QuartoKnows.com

10 9 8 7 6 5 4 3 2 1

ISBN: 978-0-7603-6069-9

Digital edition published in 2018

eISBN: 978-0-7603-6070-5

Library of Congress Cataloging-in-Publication Data is on file

Acquiring Editor: Zack Miller
Project Manager: Alyssa Lochner
Art Director: Brad Springer
Cover Designer: Emily Wiegel
Design and Layout: Silverglass Design

Front cover: The Petersen photographer photographs Petersen the photographer! Petersen staffer Eric Rickman credits Lee Blaisdell with bagging this great shot of Robert E. Petersen on the salt or the dry lakes with his big Speed Graphic Pressmaster view camera capturing a stripped-down roadster on a top speed run, likely during the late 1940s. *Petersen Photo Archive / TEN: The Enthusiast Network*
Back cover: The November 1950 *Hot Rod* cover. *Petersen Photo Archive / TEN: The Enthusiast Network*
Back flap: The famous Bob McGee '32 Ford Roadster. *Petersen Foundation collection*
Front endsheet: Two *Hot Rod* enthusiasts parked in front of Petersen Publishing Company's 1950s headquarters at 5959 Hollywood Boulevard. *Petersen Photo Archive / TEN: The Enthusiast Network*
Back endsheet: R. E. P. in front of the 1966 Chrysler Imperial built and customized for use in *The Green Hornet* TV series. *Petersen Foundation collection*

On the frontis: Herman Russell preparing to hit the track at Bonneville, circa 1950. *Petersen Photo Archive/TEN: The Enthusiast Network*
On the title page: Wally Parks waves out the window of the "Suddenly" Plymouth. *Petersen Photo Archive/TEN: The Enthusiast Network*
At right: One of many Petersen Publishing vans that supported teams at the races, on the road, or out on road tests. *Petersen Photo Archive/TEN: The Enthusiast Network*

Printed in China

We dedicate this work to those who lived the story. First and foremost,
this book is dedicated to the incomparable Margie and Robert E. Petersen for being the epic, big-
spirited people they were, for giving birth to the many movements and institutions that bear their name,
and for making an impact on everything associated with the words "hot rod." We also dedicate this book
to the unfulfilled memory of Bobby and Richie Petersen, and to all citizens of the *Hot Rod* Empire.

....

CONTENTS

THE
SOUTHERN CALIFORNIA TIMING ASSOCIATION, INC.

Presents

The First Annual

HOT ROD EXPOSITION

and

AUTOMOTIVE EQUIPMENT DISPLAY

OFFICIAL PROGRAM

HOLLYWOOD ASSOCIATES, INC.
Exposition Directors

$.244 Selling Price
.006 Sales Tax
TOTAL PRICE.............. 25c

Foreword

I first met Robert Petersen when he was the chief promoter for the Southern California Timing Association (SCTA) Hot Rod Exposition. The first of these shows, in downtown Los Angeles, took place in 1948, and they went on for a few more years after that. These events weren't based on new, stock production cars. Instead, the idea was to demonstrate the state of the art of hot rod and race car building, as well as provide a place for speed shops and performance parts companies to display their offerings.

As chief promoter for the event, Petersen was responsible for locating and booking some of the better-looking, higher-quality hot rods from around town and selling booth space to the racing-parts makers and speed shops. He was still quite young for a businessman at the time, but he was smart, tall, handsome, and easy to like. Even by this time, he had a lot of experience, having worked with the MGM Publicity department and establishing his own public relations firm, Hollywood Publicity Associates. I ended up displaying my car at the Exposition in 1949. The next year, having just opened my cam-grinding business, I wanted to be a vendor there as well, so I made plans to share a booth with Ansen Automotive.

ABOVE: A young camshaft producer named Ed Iskenderian shares his Hot Rod Expo booth with Ansen Automotive. Even though the vagaries of photo scanning and printing over the years have given this shot some strange proportions, it's still an amazing look at the earliest days of the speed parts industry. All of this vintage speed equipment is worth a fortune today; Ed is the mop-headed gent third from left. *Ed Iskenderian collection*

OPPOSITE: Robert E. Petersen's first real foray into the hot rod publishing and events businesses began with the creation of the original SCTA Hot Rod Exposition held in Los Angeles in 1948. The birth of *Hot Rod* magazine ultimately coincided with this. *Petersen Foundation collection*

1950 Catalogue
Twenty-Five Cents
Copyright 1950

ABOVE: Ignore what may be six-decades-old coffee stains: this is the cover of the performance parts catalog that Leon Cook, John Athan, and Ed Iskenderian put together for the 1950 Hot Rod Expo. *Ed Iskenderian collection*

RIGHT: Isky Racing Cams' first ad in *Hot Rod*. Ed didn't hear about the new magazine in time to get an ad in the first issue, but this piece ran in the second issue. The company was a staunch supporter of *Hot Rod* for decades to follow. *Ed Iskenderian collection*

OPPOSITE: A big day for a little guy: Ed Iskenderian's Ford V-8–powered Model T "Turtledeck" hot rod roadster appeared on the cover of *Hot Rod*'s fifth issue in June 1948. The feature on the car inside the magazine was one page long, containing just three photos. *Petersen Photo Archive/TEN: The Enthusiast Network*

Naturally, I wanted to put on a good front at the show, even though I was just a young guy and didn't really know what I was doing. I assembled a bunch of materials—photographs and other graphics stuff designed by my friend and fellow hot rodder John Athan— and I wanted to make it into some kind of brochure or catalog to hand out to the people attending the show who might be interested in my products. But I didn't know how, and the show was only a few days away. Luckily, one night while I was at my shop (on West Jefferson Avenue in Los Angeles, across the street from Vic Edelbrock's business) trying to figure out what to do, a young man walked into my office and introduced himself as Leon Cook, an artist who worked in advertising and publicity. He said he did sales brochures and things like that, so I showed him what I had and told him what I needed, figuring there was no way it could be done in 72 hours. He said he knew how to do the layouts, and he had people who could work overtime to get it done and print it fast enough to have it ready for the show. And he did it!

I had also become even more aware of Petersen when he launched *Hot Rod* magazine in 1948. I was disappointed not to have known about it in time to buy an ad in the first issue, but I was able to place an ad in the second issue. That first ad was very small, just a couple of column inches, and I remember it cost me thirty dollars. I'll never forget Petersen coming to my apartment himself to pick up the check for those first ads; he'd sometimes stick around

HOT ROD
Magazine

Ed Iskenderian in his T Roadster JUNE, 1948

at my place and use the phone to make sales calls and book other appointments around town. Imagine that: this guy who ultimately became a hugely successful publisher—and a very wealthy guy—coming to my house in person to pick up a thirty-dollar check!

I couldn't believe it when, for the fifth issue of *Hot Rod* (June 1948), he decided to put my Model T roadster on the magazine's cover as "Hot Rod of the Month." That was a big deal for a little guy with a home-built hot rod.

Most of the responses I received to those first ads came in the form of letters from interested readers. I wrote back to every one of them, dictating correspondence to a hired part-time typist. I offered them the "magazine discount rate"—ten dollars off, so only twenty dollars instead of thirty to grind a cam. Advertising in *Hot Rod* was successful for us over the years. Later on, particularly in the 1960s as our company really grew, we were advertising every month with a full-page ad, just like Chevrolet, Ford, and the big car companies. It cost a lot of money, but it ended up being worth it. We worked hard to come up with a new ad every month, featuring different products, and the race-winning cars and drivers that used our stuff. And I'll never forget those Petersen Publishing Company fishing trips! I love to fish and wouldn't miss one.

Petersen and Wally Parks, *Hot Rod*'s first editor, and National Hot Rod Association founder, didn't know it at the time, but those SCTA Hot Rod Expositions (and some other hot rod shows that

ABOVE: Iskenderian, SEMA's founding president, left, with Petersen, middle, and *Hot Rod* publisher Ray Brock, right, at the SEMA trade show in the late 1960s. *Petersen Photo Archive/ TEN: The Enthusiast Network*

OPPOSITE: One of many memorable Petersen Publishing Company fishing trips, few of which Ed Iskenderian missed. Isky is crouched in the front row, at right, with Petersen (also quite the fisherman) immediately behind him, and longtime PPC editorial staffer Tom Medley (hat, glasses, and multiple autographed shirt) just behind Mr. P. *Petersen Photo Archive/ TEN: The Enthusiast Network*

Ed "The Camfather" Iskenderian today, at age 97, still behind the counter, remembers Robert E. Petersen well. He still speaks highly of him, crediting him with "really kicking off" the whole hot rodding movement. *Mel Stone photo*

Petersen was involved with) were the forerunners of today's Specialty Equipment Market Association (SEMA) annual aftermarket industry trade show in Las Vegas. Petersen was involved with the evolution of our contemporary hot rod shows.

There's no question that hot rodding, drag racing, and Bonneville-style land-speed racing would have become huge no matter who was involved in the early days. But Robert Petersen understood them, and, ultimately, *Hot Rod* and Petersen Publishing really kicked off the whole deal.

Ed Iskenderian

Ed Iskenderian

Preface
—GIGI CARLETON

"I originally signed on for a six-week temp job, and never left!"

I'm so proud to have worked for Margie and Robert E. Petersen, my employers, for more than forty years. I would have never stayed in any job that long if it wasn't fun, and if I wasn't working for people whom were so smart, so loyal, fair minded, and had big hearts.

Mr. Petersen—the Boss—had great ideas, a terrific smile, and a twinkle in his eye, especially when he would come into the office and ask, "Guess what we're going to do today!" It was always a surprise, and it could be anything: "I just bought the world-famous Scandia restaurant on the Sunset Strip and you are going to help Margie and me oversee it," or "Peter Ueberroth talked me into being the Shooting Sports Commissioner for the 1984 Los Angeles Olympics, and you are going to be my chief of staff and help me run it," or "I'm going to start a charter aviation business at the Van Nuys Airport." And, believe me, there were many more surprises like that over four decades. It didn't matter that I had never done any of these jobs before. One of Mr. Petersen's mottos was "Just do it, and do it now." He knew I was up to nearly any challenge, and that I could do it for him, and would. Never mind that we were usually publishing thirty to fifty magazine titles when these surprises came about.

No matter whether at a party, at home, or at the office, right arm and confidante Gigi Carleton (far right) was seldom far away from Margie and Robert E. Petersen. *Petersen Photo Archive/TEN: The Enthusiast Network*

I'll never forget that I had to categorize all of his mail—he never wanted anything thrown out before he read it. That included solicitation junk mail and anything from which he might glean even the smallest business or promotional idea. As you can see from the above examples, Mr. P. was a brilliant idea generator. He was always looking for something new he could learn about, or that might present a business opportunity. He was a well-credentialed wine connoisseur, a world-famous gun collector, an avid outdoorsman, and a world traveler. And I should also mention that the Petersens were extremely philanthropic, generously donating and supporting an incalculable variety of organizations and causes.

Besides being a magazine publisher, he was a great teacher and loved to share his knowledge and skills regarding anything he knew about. Sometimes, when we were at the world-famous Petersen Automotive Museum in Los Angeles previewing a new exhibit, we would see what we all now call a "collector car." He either knew about it, or had once owned it, and would tell a great and often funny story about that car.

The Petersens and I spent so much of our lives together that we became much more than friends—they treated me wonderfully, and I think of them every day.

Among his many accomplishments, the greatest were becoming a father to his two young sons, Robert and Richard (whom we all knew, naturally, as Bobby and Richie), who died tragically in a plane crash in 1975. And he was the founding benefactor and principle creator of the aforementioned Petersen Automotive Museum. Not to mention launching *Hot Rod* magazine, the Petersen Publishing Company, and a handful of other business endeavors.

I'm pleased to welcome you to this book, to share so many photographs and other great memories from their personal and professional lives, the beginnings of the hot rod movements, and the growth of specialty publishing in America.

Mr. and Mrs. Petersen lived large, epic lives, and will never be replaced, nor will they ever be forgotten.

Gigi Carleton

Gigi Carleton

Preface

—BRUCE MEYER

Growing up in the heart of Los Angeles in the late 1940s was magical—it was Mayberry, Pleasantville, and Ozzie & Harriet all rolled into one! Dreams did come true for me as a car-loving youngster, and what determined my future and passion in life were two magazines: the Scouting magazine *Boy's Life* and Petersen Publishing's *Hot Rod*. Later in life, my path serendipitously crossed that of Robert E. Petersen on a regular basis. We lived just blocks apart, and we both served and supported two organizations together: The Board of Trustees of the Natural History Museum of Los Angeles, and the Young Presidents' Organization. We were friends, but I held Pete up on a higher level, based on admiration of this man's innate brilliance, creativity, and generosity. As you will read in this book, he was an entirely self-made man, driven by his passions for guns, hunting, flying, yachting, scuba diving, art collecting, and, of course, automobiles.

Most of all, Pete loved the "deal." When a real estate broker presented him the abandoned Ohrbach's department store building on the corner of Fairfax Avenue and Wilshire Boulevard, it started his creative wheels turning. He'd previously launched an automotive

Bruce Meyer, longtime chairman and majordomo of the Petersen Automotive Museum, with Mrs. Petersen and Jay Leno. *Petersen Foundation collection*

museum called Motorama, which had proved unsuccessful. He approached the Natural History Museum of Los Angeles Board and convinced them that they needed the Ohrbach's building for an automobile museum, as they had cars in storage with opportunities to display and share them.

Working with Pete was very special, and I can see why his teams and businesses were so successful—he truly delegated work and made each individual responsible and accountable. But that twinkle in his eye was all business and he kept watch on the details. Yet no matter, we were underway and I was voted in as the new venture's first chairman of the board.

The Petersen Automotive Museum became everything that people thought R. E. P. was, and the name Petersen was out in front and in lights—he and his glamorous wife Margie, an internationally known model, loved that. We had galas, special events, and fundraisers for their multitude of charities.

At first, Pete wasn't a hands-on hot rodder. He had worked as a photographer and PR rep at MGM Studios when a group of young enthusiasts went out to the Southern California dry lakes—El Mirage and Muroc—and titles like *Harper's* needed someone with a camera to help capture the cars and romance of the movement. He and a friend went to the races together and assembled a newsletter, which became *Hot Rod* magazine.

Promotion came naturally to Pete, so the hardware that drew him in were special cars that people enjoyed; custom creations by innovators such as George Barris, Ed "Big Daddy" Roth, and Dean Jeffries ranked high on his list. Ultimately, the cars that attracted him were bespoke French cars from the '30s and so on—and of course movie and movie-star cars. To the Bonneville and racing enthusiasts, these weren't real performance cars, but show cars. And, truth be told, Pete was not a hardcore mechanic or racer (although he did make some runs at Bonneville—once on a motorcycle!). He knew great cars when he saw them, though, and he knew how to promote, and what kind of magazines the market desired.

All in all, specialty publishing in America would have never become what it is without the Petersens. Other small publishing companies sprang up and attempted to compete and capitalize on the trends that Pete identified; several of those titles or companies didn't last, either going out of business or being acquired by what became the Petersen Publishing Company. Fortunately, we have so many great magazine titles such as *Hot Rod*, *Hot Rod Deluxe*, *Motor Trend*, and many others, plus the world-class Petersen Automotive Museum, to celebrate Pete and Margie's memorable lives and legacy. It's my honor to have known them and to have worked alongside them for so many years.

Bruce Meyer

MOTOR trend

the magazine for a motoring world

TWENTY FIVE CENTS

Introduction

Mr. and Mrs. Robert E. Petersen were epic people.

There's no other way to describe them. They birthed and developed the juggernaut of American specialty publishing, had vision on so many levels, and employed thousands of people directly and indirectly. They were born of simple means, yet became multimillionaires. Everything Mr. and Mrs. Petersen did in their lives had a bigness to it, a quality we shouldn't confuse with being showy.

They were generous with their hearts, and often with their considerable wealth. Proud Americans. Sophisticated, yet down to earth. Cultured without being snobby. Charitable, loyal, honest, hard working, and well traveled. Their list of friends and acquaintances included a long list of movers and shakers, politicians and movie stars, hot rodders, racers, socialites, and captains of industry. They lived well but also suffered immense personal tragedy.

When I was a young guy first discovering cars, it seemed like I subscribed to every title produced by the Petersen Publishing Company (PPC). Of course I didn't, but my mailman brought a PPC magazine to my family doorstep at least twice a week, most of them recognizable titles: *Motor Trend, Sports Car Graphic, Car Craft, Petersen's*

ABOVE: Mr. and Mrs. Petersen were a dashing couple wherever they were. The accomplished duo beam during *Hot Rod*'s twenty-fifth anniversary party in 1973. *Petersen Photo Archive/TEN: The Enthusiast Network*

OPPOSITE: *Motor Trend* was the young Petersen Publishing Company's second major title, launched in 1949. Mr. Petersen shot the cover photo himself; your author began reading *Motor Trend* in the mid-1960s. *Petersen Photo Archive/TEN: The Enthusiast Network*

Photographic, and, of course, *Hot Rod*, the one that started it all. I also picked up many of the annuals, books, yearbooks, and special one-offs produced by the company.

As that kid, then young adult, reading all those Petersen titles, I dreamed of being a car writer and road tester at *Motor Trend* or *Sports Car Graphic*. How cool would that be—road-testing cars, writing stories, taking pictures, and hanging out with fascinating people in interesting places? Exotic travel. International auto shows. Driving fast in the newest and hottest hardware.

The guys who made those magazines became my heroes. The late, great Eric Dahlquist was one of the key mentors in my life and career. My friend, Kevin Smith, along with nearly a dozen others along the PPC trail—John Christy, David E. Davis Jr., Len Frank, Chuck Koch, Fred M. H. Gregory, Jim McGraw, John Lamm, Bob Nagy, Chuck Queener, C. Van Tune, racing writer extraordinaire Jerry Titus—all had their influence on me.

I got my chance to live the life of a motor journalist in late 1997. After quitting my "real job" to become a freelance writer and photographer, I joined the *Motor Trend* staff, thanks to an invite from then–Editor in Chief C. Van Tune. I'd never been on a production staff, and I didn't know much about the production, advertising, distribution, and marketing sides of the publishing business—I figured I'd give it a try for a while and see what I could learn.

"A while" lasted fifteen years. In the end, I became executive editor of *Motor Trend* and ran my own title as editor of *Motor Trend Classic*. I never worked for Mr. and Mrs. Petersen directly, since they had sold their company in 1996, but I knew "the Boss" through the business, of course, and the fact that our *Motor Trend* editorial offices remained in the Petersen Building on Wilshire Boulevard in Los Angeles. I saw Mr. and Mrs. P. around the building all the time, at the Pebble Beach Concours d'Elegance, and at nearly every event or gallery opening held at their baby, the Petersen Automotive Museum.

Like Frank Sinatra, Robert E. Petersen garnered a number of nicknames over time: "Bob," "Pete," "R. E. P.," "the Boss," "the Chairman," and "the King of Hot Rod Publishing." He wore them all well. *Petersen Foundation collection*

Mr. Petersen read every page of each new issue of *Motor Trend* the day it was published. Something I had written must have made an impression: we had a friendly acquaintance, and every time we met in the elevators we'd wind up chatting about Hollywood cars, cars in pop culture, classics, and historic and collector cars. I never worked for *Hot Rod* as a staffer, although I contributed later as a freelancer.

It was my honor to be the last journalist to interview him formally before Mr. Petersen's passing. I remember him telling me of the days when he and some of the staff would set up their trailer at the drag races or Bonneville, selling *Hot Rod* to the crowd, at twenty-five cents a copy. "Whether we had steak or a hamburger, and whether we slept in a motel room or in the car depended on how many magazines we sold that day." Imagine.

During my tenure at *Motor Trend*, I met and befriended my partner in this book, Gigi Carleton. Gigi served as Mr. and Mrs. P.'s personal secretary and administrative manager for more than four decades; she is now president of the Margie and Robert E. Petersen Foundation. Her love and respect for these special people, plus her skillful and diligent management of the Petersens' personal archive of photos and documents, have made this book possible. That, and PPC's archive of the many millions of photographs used to assemble all those magazines, now owned and operated by The Enthusiast Network (TEN).

There is some confusion about Mr. Petersen's first name or, more correctly, his nicknames. Many refer to him as "Bob" Petersen, which isn't so unusual since "Bob" is a common short form of Robert. "R. E. P." is also a good reference. People who were closer to him or worked for him called him "Pete," and I believe he copped to this more comfortably than "Bob." Gigi most often calls him "Mr. P." or "The Boss." To me, he was always Mr. Petersen.

You couldn't find more committed and engaged automotive enthusiasts than the Petersens. They built a serious, big-game car collection. They drove, showed, and enjoyed their great cars, and they knew everything about them. The Petersens founded and launched two significant car museums, spending tens of millions of dollars to keep them going. They also donated cars to support the museums' goals of educating the world about how society, culture, history, and technology interact within what is known as the *automotive sphere.*

To think it all began with a tall, good-looking kid from East L.A. who loved cars, speed, and photography; who recognized that racing and rodding were underserved audiences that needed a voice; and who then launched an innovative little car magazine, thus giving birth to the *Hot Rod* Empire.

Matt Stone

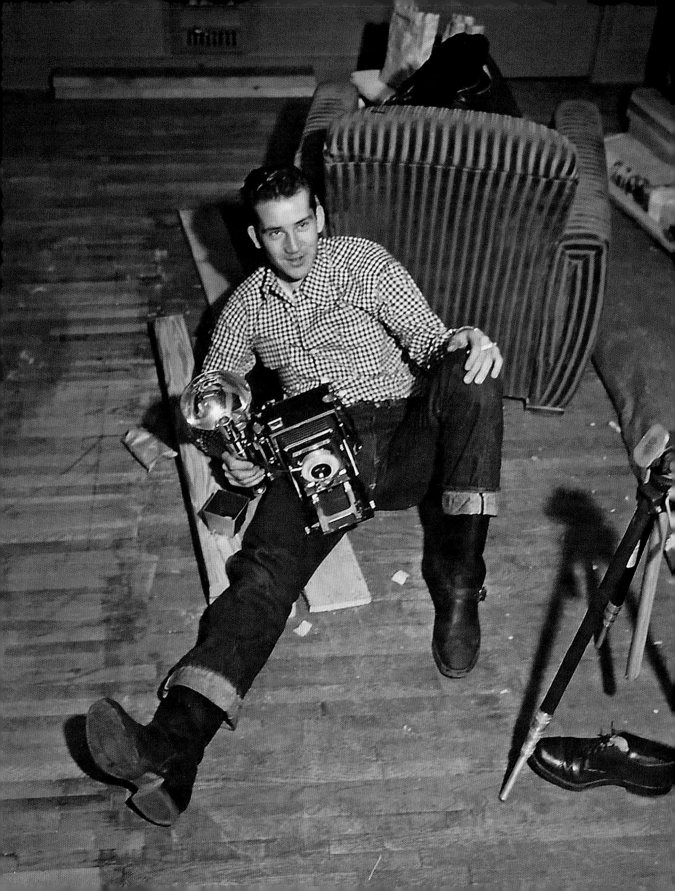

1

Meet Pete—A Star Is Born

Robert Einar Petersen was born to Mr. and Mrs. Einar Petersen (of Danish descent, and very proud of their Viking heritage) in Los Angeles, California, on September 10, 1926. He was an average young man with interests that were typical for a guy growing up in the 1940s in Southern

California: cars, motorcycles, guns, and girls. His mother passed away when he was young and he ended up living with his father, an automotive/truck mechanic and machinist, in Barstow, California, a desert community northwest of L.A. There's a story that young Petersen was a high school dropout, but this isn't true: he graduated from Barstow Union High School in 1942, although his high school principal told him he'd "never amount to anything"—an unfortunate comment from a senior educator, and way off the mark considering that the tall, handsome kid ended up on the Forbes 400 list of the wealthiest people in America. As a teen, he held a few jobs, including one as a dishwasher at Wolverton's Home Café. Cars, guns, and dates cost money, after all.

After high school, Robert (now nicknamed "Pete") joined the Army Air Corps (AAC), an early version of the United States Air Force. We say he joined, though it's not clear if he enlisted or was drafted. He joined the AAC's photography corps and was assigned as a photography

OPPOSITE: Pete was a leggy young man. He's seen here with his trademark Speed Graphic view camera, the shooter's weapon of choice long before 35mm roll film cameras became prevalent or popular. The large 4x5 negative gave unmatched sharpness, but these cameras were heavy and cumbersome to use. Note the heavy-duty tripod in lower right of frame. *Petersen Foundation collection*

technician. Stationed in Montana on active duty, Pete never left the state to serve in actual combat. We don't believe he chose recon photography as his specialty, although it appears he liked it. As he often told it, "they handed me a camera and told me to go up in that airplane and learn how to take pictures." He was honorably discharged in 1945.

Young guys liked cars. And many of them liked the speed, noise, and sense of danger that went along with fast cars and racing. Petersen was one of those guys.

The seeds of American hot rodding were planted as far back as the 1920s (well documented in Dean Batchelor's definitive book on the subject, *American Hot Rod*), but this burgeoning movement really took off after World War II. Military service had given tens of thousands of young men an appreciation for all things motorized and mechanical, and they had learned wartime skills such as welding, machining, metal fabrication, and mechanical repair. They all had some mustering-out

OPPOSITE: Corpsman Petersen (top left) with a few of the other servicemen in this Army Air Corps photo unit, circa 1943–44. *Petersen Foundation collection*

ABOVE: A typical dry lake racing scene: a gang of young guys in jeans and T-shirts, hundreds of hot rods, and miles of ultra-smooth lakebed on which to go fast with nothing in the way. The real essence of hot rodding. This is the famous Bob McGee '32 Ford Roadster. *Petersen Foundation collection*

This stripped-down Model A roadster gave up its four-banger for a much larger and longer Cadillac V-16 engine, which necessitated some major reworking of the chassis and firewall areas to make it fit; the rest of the scene is typical of the earliest days of dry lakes racing: a group of dusty and somewhat tired-looking guys milling about, checking out the hottest and fastest hardware. *Author collection*

pay in their pockets, and old Ford "Lizzies" (Model Ts) and Model As were available used—and dirt cheap. A Model T that ran well cost five, ten, or twenty bucks, while the more powerful Model As went for a little more. Henry Ford's hot-performing, low-cost V-8 engine—the famous Ford flathead—was launched in 1932. With a Ford Roadster stripped of more cumbersome components (headlights, fenders, running boards, and often windshields), this engine offered plenty of power; the same was true for a lightweight Model T.

By the late 1940s, hot rodding had expanded further: unsanctioned street racing, organized drag racing, and "top-speed" racing on Southern California's dry lakes—regions in the high deserts north of Los Angeles, such as Muroc and El Mirage—all contributed to the growth of this new American sport. Somewhere along the way, drivers started calling these modified cars "hot rods" or "gow jobs." We should be pleased that the former moniker stuck—somehow *"Gow Job Magazine"* doesn't have the same ring as *Hot Rod*. Not to mention *Popular Hot Rodding* could have been born as *Popular Gow Jobbing*—not exactly lyrical.

Hot rodding couldn't be called a career—yet. With school and the military behind him, young Petersen needed a "real job." Pete's father knew someone at Metro-Goldwyn-Mayer (MGM) studios, and he suggested that his son apply there for a job after the war. His natural interest in writing and photography, in addition to his recent military experience in the latter, gave Petersen a foot in the door to be hired

Team photo of the MGM Publicity Department corps, circa 1946. Petersen is in the second from the back row, second from left. Richard Anderson, later known as a character actor in TV and film, is second from back row, far right; he was one of Petersen's longtime friends. *Petersen Foundation collection*

It's easy to spot Petersen at this 1947 gathering of the Throttlers Hot Rod Club: Pete is the tall, big-haired guy sixth from left; he appears to have his knee lifted and resting on the tire of the second car in. This photo defines the look of what are now called "traditional hot rods." *Petersen Foundation collection*

as a messenger. He was smart and a quick study, demonstrating his skills with people and a camera, and he soon become a full-fledged publicist. While at MGM, he met many of the brightest stars of the day, including Marilyn Monroe and the billionaire aviator, inventor, and movie producer Howard Hughes. Petersen was writing press releases and media pieces for a variety of MGM stars and film projects, clacking them out on his trusty cast-iron, black-bodied Underwood typewriter.

After Petersen and a few of the other young associates were swept up in a round of layoffs at MGM in 1946, they decided to hang out their own shingle and see if they could make it in the PR game. Together they formed Hollywood Publicity Associates (HPA). It was about this time that several influences collided to change automotive and hot-rodding history. In mid-1947, HPA was engaged by the Southern California Timing Association (SCTA), a recently formed race sanctioning body, to promote and stage the first-ever Hot Rod Exposition, a car and trade show intended to show off the style, technology, and speed of modern hot rods; it would also serve as an outlet for a growing number of speed parts makers to show and sell their wares. Petersen and HPA business partner Robert Lindsay put together publicity for the massive event, scheduled for January 1948. Along with Wally Parks, one of the SCTA's founding fathers, they divined that "this hot-rodding thing" had become, and would continue to be, a major sporting, cultural, and business force. This became particularly true, first in Southern California and then nationally.

OPPOSITE: The start of something big: the first issue of *Hot Rod* magazine, published January 1948, featured Regg Schlemmer's "track-nosed" Model T roadster, fresh off a record-setting run at El Mirage in October 1947, with driver Eddie Hulse at the wheel. His top speed that day was 136.05 miles per hour, pretty brave considering the tire and braking technology of the day. Car owner Schlemmer was interviewed in that first issue. *Petersen Photo Archive/TEN: The Enthusiast Network*

HOT ROD *Magazine*

VOL. 1, NO. 1 • • • PRICE 25¢   WORLD'S MOST COMPLETE HOT ROD COVERAGE   JANUARY 1948

HOT ROD OF THE MONTH

Sitting in the driver's seat is Eddie Hulse, who, a few moments after this picture was taken, drove number 668, to set a new SCTA record for Class C roadsters. Hulse, a native Californian, nosed out Randy Shinn, a long-time top honor holder for the RC Class. Shinn's old record was 129.40 in a channeled Mercury T.

Keeping the Car Out Front by George Riley—Page 10

The Pierson Brothers' famous
'34 Ford coupe being pushed
to the line at the lakes, ready
for another run. Note the
makeshift timing and scoring
tower just behind the crowd.
Petersen Foundation collection

There was no journal or publishing voice for this nascent movement, but Petersen and Lindsay were tuned into voices that nobody else could hear. There were already magazines dedicated to cars. England's *Autocar* first published an issue in 1895, and *Road & Track* had launched in America in 1947. But these established titles focused primarily on the new car market and motorsports. Hot rodding wasn't yet meaningful on any existing publisher's radar. All of this spawned an idea for the twenty-two-year-old Robert E. Petersen: he saw an opportunity for announcing big news at the upcoming January 1948 Hot Rod Expo.

Petersen and Lindsay conspired to launch a new magazine dedicated to the cars, people, and places of the hot rod movement. In their minds, there was no question about what to call it: *Hot Rod* magazine. In advance of the Hot Rod Expo, they raised some working capital (some sources say $200, others claim it was $400), wrote several stories and shot dozens of photos (employing his trusty Underwood and Speed Graphic–type press cameras), and printed five thousand copies of the magazine to see if anyone was interested. The first issue, dated January 1948, was published just in time for the Hot Rod Expo. In fact, an ad promoting the show was on the back page of the magazine.

Touting a "worldwide annual subscription rate" of three dollars, the newborn magazine was initially published by The Hot Rod Publishing Company (112 South La Brea Avenue, Los Angeles 36, California, which was Petersen's apartment).

The editor's column of that first volume 1, number 1 of *Hot Rod* promised readers that:

Hot Rod *is published to inform and entertain those interested in automobiles whose bodies and engines have been rebuilt in the quest for better performance and appearance. In this publication, readers will find a chance to air their views, ask questions (and get the answers), read about racing and timing meets and automobile shows, see the latest in engine and body designs, enjoy entertaining fiction and see engine parts displayed with what we call the "feminine touch."*

In today's more culturally aware world, some might consider that "feminine touch" comment as a harbinger of the objectification of women. From the beginning, *Hot Rod* featured what were then commonly called "cheesecake" photos of attractive young women holding, pointing to, or posed with hot rod speed parts. That section was named "Parts with Appeal." Initially, these photos were ever-so-slightly sexy, yet modest, never trashy, though as time passed the photos got racier, often filling full pages with smiling, bikini-clad women. The discussion of each component, be it a carburetor, intake manifold, exhaust system, or wheels, always included a brief bio of the model, her interests, education, and vocation (if she wasn't a professional model).

Wally Parks, SCTA head and later the founder of the National Hot Rod Association (NHRA), wound up as *Hot Rod*'s first official editor, though he didn't appear as such until November 1949; his first title was as the magazine's "technical advisor." Petersen and Lindsay listed themselves on that first masthead as associate editors, although they were essentially the co-editors of the magazine at the beginning.

Things like the Hot Rod Exposition and *Hot Rod* magazine were utterly new ideas. Was the vision that Petersen and Lindsay had for a new magazine and publishing company merely a one-time pursuit, destined to remain a flash in their personal pan? Or was it the kernel of something much larger, with a real future?

Return postage guaranteed:
HOT ROD MAGAZINE
112 South La Brea
Los Angeles 36, Calif.

Sec. 562, P.L.&R.
U. S. POSTAGE
PAID
Los Angeles, Calif.
Permit No. 14097

SOUTHERN CALIFORNIA TIMING ASSOCIATION INC.

Announces

The First Annual

Automotive Equipment Display

and

Hot Rod Exposition

JAN. 23rd - 24th - 25th

At The National Guard Armory - - - Exposition Park
Los Angeles

Drive Carefully . . . Save A Life

The premier issue of *Hot Rod* wasn't intended as a program for the 1948 Hot Rod Expo, but it plugged the upcoming event inside the issue and on the back cover. This was the first of many hot rod exhibits and trade shows that Robert E. Petersen worked on. *Petersen Photo Archive/TEN: The Enthusiast Network*

Petersen Publishing Company Goes from 0 to 60

Both *Hot Rod* magazine and the Hot Rod Exposition were successes. At the time, the Expo likely seemed the more significant of Petersen's two undertakings. He's been quoted as saying that they produced the magazine as something of a whim for their friends in the hobby, not really knowing if it would go anywhere. We now know the answer.

The expo was a huge success with the burgeoning speed parts industry and those in the growing hobby. The organizers immediately planned another such event in 1949. (These early shows were the first of what became a core part of Petersen's working life, as he went on to play a significant role in launching many major performance industry shows and conventions throughout his career.) The 1949 Hot Rod Expo increased in size and scope, with more hot rods on display, expanded news coverage, and double the show days added to the schedule.

This expo also premiered a feature that's still a popular attraction at car shows today: a select group of hot rod builders gathered to build something live throughout the show's nine-day schedule. In 1949, they applied their skills to build out a pair of '32 Ford hot rods as the crowd watched and learned.

OPPOSITE: Petersen and Lindsay worked hard to fill their first Hot Rod Exposition with some of Southern California's better rod and race cars, and this photo proves that they did. The car front left became the cover subject of *Hot Rod* issue 1-1, and the rest of the photo shows an interesting combination of the different hot rod and race car styles that were already setting the trends in 1948. Wonder where they all are today? *Petersen Foundation collection*

HOT ROD *Magazine*

November - 1947

25¢

The Cover Car - PAGE 5

The first issue of *Hot Rod* (with a print run of ten thousand copies) sold out quickly, and subscription orders came flowing in. Plans were immediately made to publish the second issue, and that February 1948 cover featured Keith Landrigan's LaSalle-powered Ford Roadster hot rod. The editorial content continued to evolve as the magazine gained credibility and voice. Some of the subjects were street and show rods, others showed stripped-down rods competing at the dry lakes or on racetracks.

Two covers worth noting from that first year included the June 1948 cover, featuring cam-grinding legend Ed Iskenderian's Model T rod, and the October 1948 cover with a handsome action photo taken on the grounds of USC of rodder/racer/builder Bob McGee and his seminal 1932 Ford Deuce highboy roadster. This car was considered among the most definitive examples—then and now—of a traditional hot rod, and it is currently owned by Petersen Museum board member Bruce Meyer. Cover images in 1948 were black-and-white photographs, framed by red bands at top and bottom containing the magazine logotype, cover lines, issue date, price, and so forth. Color photos didn't come along until 1949.

As the company and the magazine grew, so did the staff. Beyond founders Petersen and Lindsay, the next employee was Tom Medley, joining in time for the February 1948 issue; he was soon followed by future (and, officially, first) editor, Wally Parks. Among his many talents, Medley was a gifted illustrator and cartoonist, and *Hot Rod* became famous for his cartoons containing the trials, tribulations, and adventures of his mythical character, Stroker McGurk.

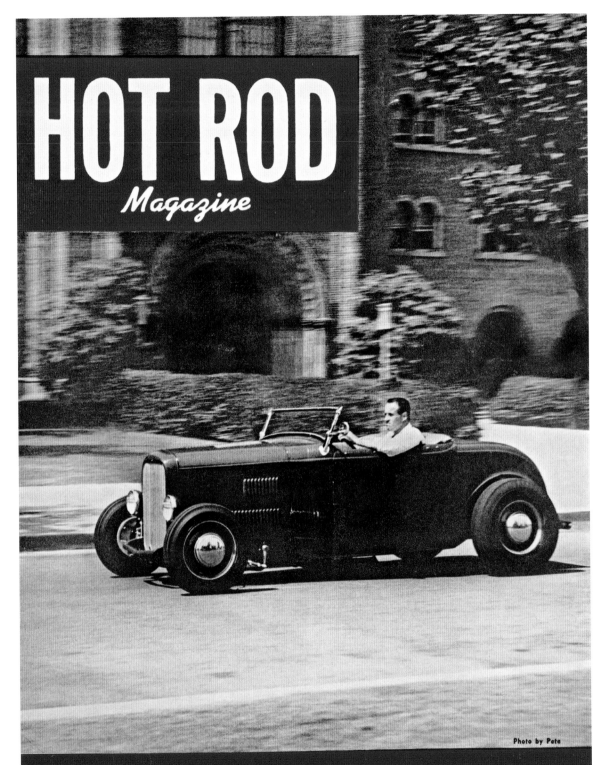

HOT ROD
Magazine

Photo by Pete

Bob McGee on the S.C. Campus   OCTOBER, 1948   **25c**

Working hard on the salt. Editor Wally Parks, left, holding movie camera; a shirtless staff editor Dick Day in the middle, and R. E. P. on the right, wielding a camera and battery-pack-powered flash unit. The Ford F-1 panel truck was painted bright red and white, *Hot Rod*'s official colors for many years; the guys' shirts were also bright red, with white embroidery. *Petersen Photo Archive/TEN: The Enthusiast Network*

We don't know the exact year or locale of this luau-inspired party photo of three of *Hot Rod*'s first editorial staffers, but they appear to be having fun and enjoying the famous Holmes and Kugel racer. They are, from left, Wally Parks, Tom Medley, and Robert E. Petersen. *Petersen Foundation collection*

Gray Baskerville, another longtime *Hot Rod* editor, said this about Medley and McGurk in 1998:

Except for a brief comeback bid between 1964 and 1965, Tom Medley's legendary Stroker McGurk cartoon series ended more than 40 years ago. Yet McGurk's eight-year run—starting in March 1948 and finishing with the October 1955 issue of Hot Rod—*served as a harbinger. Medley's fertile imagination predated wheelies, ram-air systems, drag chutes, blown overheads, multi-engine dragsters, sleepers, gassers and vintage tin, and aftermarket kits that didn't fit . . . see why Stroker McGurk became hot rodding's favorite foul-up?*

Even though Medley may be better known for his stewardship of *Rod & Custom* magazine, his artistic touch and sense of humor added a lot to the pages of *Hot Rod*. His illustration skills were also occasionally employed for *Hot Rod* covers instead of the more customary photographs. Medley was much more than a cartoonist: he was really a hot rodder and automotive designer who happened to use his illustration skills to display his humor and ideas.

Another major hire was Ray Brock, who joined *Hot Rod* as an editorial staffer in 1953. Brock was a tall, big-voiced guy who proved to be a natural "networker." He was also a serious and accomplished racer, having gunned the salts of Bonneville and the desert sands of Baja. He enjoyed a long career with Petersen Publishing, ultimately becoming *Hot Rod* publisher and a major force in the performance industry. His many contributions over time were significant.

Automakers liked what they saw in *Hot Rod*, but they didn't feel it directly addressed the new car-buying public. Once Petersen had built up capacity for magazine publishing, he realized that the market had room for a magazine dedicated

Looking very businesslike indeed. Ray Brock, an early and highly significant staff technical editor, was more often seen in a *Hot Rod* T-shirt or a racing suit. As he became a publishing exec later in his career, this outfit became his uniform. *Petersen Photo Archive/TEN: The Enthusiast Network*

primarily to new car buyers and advertisers, plus forms of racing not typically featured in *Hot Rod*. He worked to develop a new title to serve as "the Magazine for a Motoring World." It would include features on new cars, used cars, trends in styling and design, technology developments, racing, and automotive history.

Motor Trend's first editor was Walter A. Woron. Tasked with naming the new title, Woron's response to Petersen went something like this:

"What shall we call it?" asked Woron.

"How about *Motor Sports*?" suggested Petersen.

"That's a good name, Pete, but it doesn't tell what the magazine is," contended Woron. "Sounds too much like a racing mag. It should be something to tell what it is . . . like, the trends in motoring . . . ."

"Sure. Just turn it around. Something like *Motoring Trends*. Or *Motor Trends*. That's pretty good."

And there it was. *Motor Trend* made its newsstand debut in September 1949.

Petersen later told future *Motor Trend* editor C. Van Tune:

When I was first selling advertising in Hot Rod, *there were a lot of people who didn't like the name. They said if I called it something nice, they'd buy an ad. So I thought about that, but I determined that* Hot Rod *had its niche. I didn't want to change anything, especially the name. But I thought it'd be a good idea to start a magazine for those people who didn't like the hot-rod image. So I shot a photo of a Kurtis sports car with one of our secretaries posing with it . . . and we made up a dummy cover and inside pages. I showed it around and those people [who didn't care for* Hot Rod*] said "Yeah, I'd advertise in that!" Which is how we launched* Motor Trend.

Motor Trend was by no means the only new title created by the young, aggressive Petersen Publishing Company. It was just the beginning. Following *Motor Trend*, Petersen launched *Cycle* in 1950 to serve motorcycle enthusiasts. *Honk* was introduced in 1953 as a smaller, pocket-sized riff on *Hot Rod*, dedicated primarily to the popular customizing movements of the day. And, as drag racing and land-speed-record racing

OPPOSITE: R. E. P., left, and *Motor Trend's* first editor, Walt Woron, at right, visit the British Motors Corporation HQ and factory in the late 1950s. *Petersen Foundation collection*

LOCATION, LOCATION, LOCATION

More titles, more business, and more employees meant a need for more space. What would in 1956 become Petersen Publishing Company made its first of many moves to new headquarters not long after its founding. The La Brea Avenue address listed in *Hot Rod*'s first issue was actually Petersen's apartment at the time. In the middle of 1948 came a move to nearby 7164 Melrose Avenue. This was followed by a short stint at 548 South San Vicente Avenue, another property in the "mid-Wilshire" area of Los Angeles. By mid-1950, the company had settled in a slightly larger office at 1015 La Cienega Boulevard.

The next move housed the company through the 1950s: 5959 Hollywood Boulevard in Hollywood. The building was, appropriately, a former car dealership with great frontage on Hollywood Boulevard and lots of glass up front. At last there was sufficient room to accommodate the company's continuing growth. The property looked nice, too, and photos of it appeared in many issues of PPC magazines over time with all manner of famous cars and enthusiasts parked in front of it.

It's interesting to trace the company's evolution through the old photos of signage on the various buildings it inhabited. We learn, for example, that it was not originally named "Petersen Publishing Company." The first entity was called The Hot Rod Publishing Company, followed by Trend Publications, then *Motor Trend* Publications, and Trend Inc. throughout the late 1940s and into the early 1950s. The "Place That Pete Built" formally became the Petersen Publishing Company (PPC) with the June 1956 issue of *Hot Rod*.

ABOVE: At the time called *Motor Trend* Publications, Petersen's office location at 1015 La Cienega Boulevard in Los Angeles. Check out the handsome pair of early '50s Fords on the right side of the photo, and also the mid-1940s Ford Woodie at far left. The name of the woman standing on the front steps is unknown. *Petersen Photo Archive/TEN: The Enthusiast Network*

OPPOSITE: Longtime PPC readers have seen this shot before because it's one of the few closeups showing the young company's "5959" headquarters on Hollywood Boulevard. The building had formerly been lettered "Trend, Inc.," but now it's boldly Petersen Publishing, with seven magazines proudly listed (*Teen* being the only nonautomotive title). The two guys in the channeled '32 roadster, like so many during that time, likely drove up and asked the receptionist, "Can we get our car in your magazine?" So, somebody sent Rick and a camera to the rear parking lot to shoot a magazine-worthy Deuce from northern California. Other frames on the roll show them pulling sleeping bags and camping gear out of the trunk. Unfortunately, the names of these enthusiastic hot rodders are unknown. *Petersen Photo Archive/TEN: The Enthusiast Network*

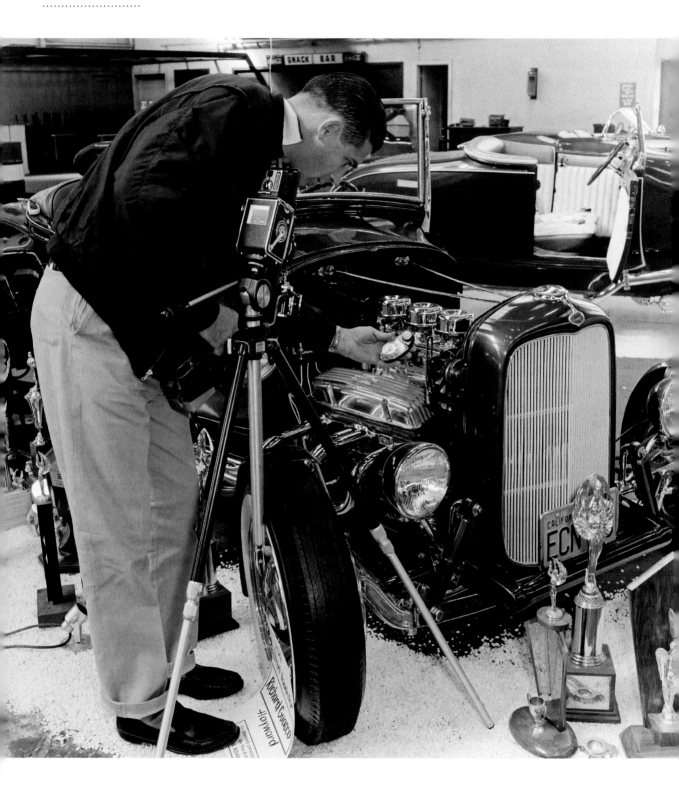

became more organized, *Car Craft* morphed out of *Honk* (which was discontinued) to better serve those enthusiasts, particularly the do-it-yourself racer and builder. *Rod & Custom* made its debut in 1955 as another "pocket-sized" magazine. (These smaller magazines were nicknamed the "little pages," their 7⅞-inch height and 10½-inch full-spread width intended to fit easily in the back pocket of a pair of Levi's.)

With transport titles rolling out at an increasing pace, Petersen turned his attention to other pursuits that focused on niche enthusiast audiences. As the company approached its tenth anniversary, he launched *Guns & Ammo,* a new title dedicated to weaponry, another of his interests.

Photographer Bob D'Olivo was a significant addition to the Petersen staff in late 1952. The visuals in any magazine are important, especially when the owner of the company himself started out as a photographer. Cars are objects that lend themselves to visual representation, and D'Olivo was a professional photographer who brought a keen eye and artistic touch to the company's photography.

Eric Rickman was another new staff photographer that year. Often called "Rick Rickman" or "E. Rick Man," he and D'Olivo formed the foundation of the Petersen Photographic Services, with D'Olivo as manager and Rickman the all-around staff shooter. Both had considerable command of the mechanics of photography and of their photo equipment, with an eye for what a given article needed. Although dozens of talented photographers joined Petersen

ABOVE: First a freelance contributor, then a staffer, Eric Rickman brought strong photography skills to *Hot Rod.* He was often bylined as E. Rickman, E. Rick Man, or just Rick. *Petersen Photo Archive/ TEN: The Enthusiast Network*

OPPOSITE: A studious Bob D'Olivo setting up and metering an ideal engine shot. D'Olivo set a high standard for quality photography at PPC, bringing solid technical skills to his work along with a great eye. *Petersen Photo Archive/TEN: The Enthusiast Network*

HOT ROD
MAGAZINE

APRIL 1951
25c

NOW—16 MORE PAGES!

DRAG STRIPS DEVELOP PHENOMENAL SPEEDS!

Photographic's team over the years, D'Olivo and Rickman were the core talent who pioneered visual standards for all Petersen publications.

Another notable staff add in the mid-1950s was Engineering Editor Ray "Racer" Brown. He was an SAE-certified engineer, in addition to being a hands-on racer and capable writer. Brown authored many of the technical articles published in *Hot Rod*, and he also handled reader correspondence of a technical nature. He had an easy-going, conversational writing style, and some of his responses to reader letters were really funny.

Petersen and Lindsay had dissolved their partnership in 1950/51; Lindsay's final appearance on the masthead was the December 1951 issue, even though his name wasn't removed from the official company name until early 1956. The reasons for

X MARKS THE MAN

When visiting the roots and tracing the history of hot rodding, you'd be hard-pressed to find a more dyed-in-the-wool hot rodder and racer than Alex Xydias. An early dry lakes and Bonneville competitor, engine builder, writer, photographer, and filmmaker, he applied his talents to documenting his favorite things: cars and motorsports. He also founded the original So-Cal Speed Shop.

Xydias's primary partner in crime was a multitalented car freak named Dean Batchelor. Xydias and Batchelor designed and created several Bonneville streamliners that ran under the *Hot Rod* and So-Cal Speed Shop banners.

Besides his considerable car design talents, Batchelor was also an excellent photographer and writer. After a stint at PPC, he took a turn as editor of *Road & Track*, later serving as curator of the William F. Harrah collections and museum in Reno. Batchelor also authored several books, including at least three on Ferrari and what many consider to be the definitive book on hot rodding, *The American Hot Rod.*

For a time, Xydias also worked at PPC as publisher of the company's first true trade publication, *Hot Rod Industry News.* He was also deeply involved in promoting the first performance industry trade show that Petersen launched in 1967.

In the mid-1990s, Xydias teamed up with late hot rodder Pete Chapouris to reprise the SO-CAL Speed Shop brand, with shops dedicated to hot rod and race car building. The goal of this enterprise was the tangible rebirth of the notion of the "speed shop."

Xydias, a lover of fine jazz music in addition to anything with a motor, is quietly retired in Burbank, California.

BELOW: The Mercury flathead-powered Batchelor/Xydias streamliner at Bonneville in 1951. Dean Batchelor is at left, with Alex Xydias on the right; the helmeted driver is unknown. *Petersen Photo Archive/TEN: The Enthusiast Network*

OPPOSITE: Rodder, racer, and enthusiast par excellence Alex Xydias pores over magazine layouts for his PPC performance industry trade magazine. Note the great drag racing photos on the wall behind him. *Petersen Photo Archive/TEN: The Enthusiast Network*

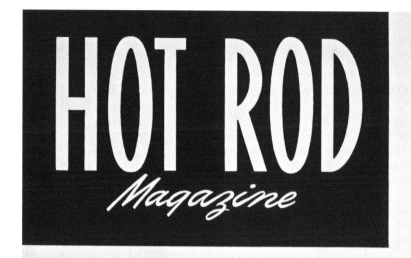

HOT ROD
Magazine

TOP RECORD BREAKER IN
BONNEVILLE SPEED TRIALS

OCTOBER 1949

T W E N T Y - F I V E   C E N T S

the partnership's end aren't clear—it's something Petersen never discussed. The final terms of their parting seem to have derived from an interesting method of negotiation. According to writer Fred M. H. Gregory's interview with Petersen some years later:

By 1951, Bob [Petersen] and Lindsay agreed to a friendly parting of the ways. They settled the ownership of the company over drinks in a Hollywood bar. Each wrote a sum on a piece of paper; the one with the high number would buy the other out for that price. Bob's $250,000 was the high bid. "In that time, it was a hell of a lot of money," Petersen said.

We don't know how touchy a subject it was, but even Gigi Carleton, his most trusted ally, never heard it discussed.

Petersen insisted on high-quality writing in his publications. Not necessarily flowery, poetic, or scholarly prose from classically trained writers or journalists, but writing that clearly showed they knew their stuff. His primary goal was to hire editors who were knowledgeable and particularly passionate about their magazine's subject, whether it was hot rods, new cars, guns, or boats. As long as an editor really knew the topics he was covering and was surrounded by others of similar mindset and passion, he believed that these enthusiast editor/writers could deliver the goods (with the help of careful copyediting and fact checking by managing editors). The formula worked like a charm: over time, Petersen Publishing has been the home of many of the world's great automotive writers. They were good with the words, but, equally important, they understood their topics and loved the game.

OPPOSITE: Yet another Xydias Streamliner on the salt makes the cover of *Hot Rod*'s October 1949 issue. That's R. E. P. in the middle, wearing the pith helmet, with Dean Bachelor in the car and Alex on the right. *Petersen Photo Archive/TEN: The Enthusiast Network*

BELOW: A scene typical of Bonneville in the early days: Herman Russell preparing to hit the track in his stripped-down roadster, with a rickety-looking "timing stand" in the background, and other cars and people milling about the starting line. Also on this November 1950 *Hot Rod* cover is the So-Cal Special Streamliner blazing the salt to a new record of over 210 miles per hour. *Petersen Photo Archive/TEN: The Enthusiast Network*

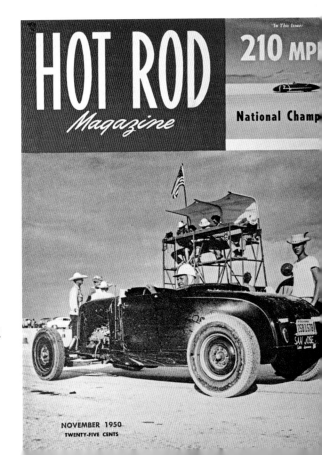

Before contemplating Petersen's next decade, we should acknowledge how much each sport evolved, as land-speed-record racing and drag racing became more organized and formalized.

Dry lakes racing in the 1940s was often promoted by local car clubs, and it was a bit of a wild-and-woolly undertaking. Timing and sanctioning methods varied greatly, as did technical and safety standards. Car classification and record keeping was something of an eyeball game, with cars often arbitrarily classified based on the cursory observation of engine modifications, engine types, body modifications, and whether a car ran a streamliner (aerodynamically optimized) body strictly for racing or more stock-looking bodywork. Ed Iskenderian recalled that, "in the beginning, we raced in whatever we were wearing, and sometimes with a hat and some old aviator goggles to keep the dust out of our eyes" with no regard for seat belts, harnesses, driving suits, gloves, or fire protection.

When The Hot Rods Ran

May 15, 1938

William Carroll

ABOVE: This great book covers the earliest days of dry lake racing; note the cover date of May 1938. The photo on the left also tells a great story: the building is the Muroc train station, and the chalkboard lists the times—both east- and westbound—that the trains run in and out of the small-town station. *Author collection*

LEFT: Proving that the boss practiced what his magazines preached, here is Mr. Petersen's timing certificate from a run he made on his BSA motorcycle, running a tick over 105 miles per hour on September 1, 1952. *Petersen Foundation collection*

OPPOSITE: *Motor Trend* also got in on the racing action at Bonneville in 1951, with this modified MG roadster; the effort was covered extensively in the pages of *MT*. That's staff photographer Bob D'Olivo wearing a hat, with his back to camera, and R. E. P. standing at the right side of the shot. *Petersen Photo Archive/TEN: The Enthusiast Network*

RIGHT: Even the Boss's car isn't safe from the *Hot Rod* staff racers. This Bonneville timing cert credits Racer Brown and Wally Park with a 103-mile-per-hour run in "Pete Petersen's Cadillac" on Sept 1, 1952. *Petersen Foundation collection*

OPPOSITE: The real backbone of the early days of *Hot Rod*, organized drag racing (and what would become Petersen Publishing Company), as embodied by these cool guys in their aviator shads: R. E. P. on the left and the even taller, lankier Wally Parks, at Bonneville. *Petersen Photo Archive/TEN: The Enthusiast Network*

CERTIFICATE OF SPEED

Clocked By *J. Otto Crocker* Electronic Timer

*T*HIS Certifies that *Wally Parks & Racer Brown* with *Pete Petersen's Cadillac* has attained a speed of *103.122* miles per hour. Date *Sept. 1, 1952* at *Bonneville Salt Flats, Utah*

Timed by *J. Otto Crocker*

Witness: _____

J. O. CROCKER OFFICIAL TIMER FOR AMERICAN POWER BOAT ASSOCIATION SOUTHERN CALIFORNIA TIMING ASSN., INC.

OFFICE AT 4749 REDLAND DRIVE • SAN DIEGO 15, CALIFORNIA

In concert with other car clubs, the SCTA elected to approach the game in a more organized manner, and established official timing meets, primarily on the Bonneville Salt Flats near Wendover, Utah. The SCTA developed better-defined classes, tech inspections, and safety standards in order to elevate the sport and make it safer and more legitimate. While top-speed racing was taking place in Florida—primarily on the long, smooth beaches of Daytona (long before the famous Daytona International Speedway was built)—Bonneville eventually became ground zero in terms of American land-speed-record racing; the salt flats there had already been employed for top-speed runs by legendary land-speed-record racers Ab Jenkins, John Cobb, and Sir Malcolm Campbell. The massive salt flats at Bonneville were smooth and fast, with no networks of roads or buildings, so it was a logical location for speed runs. Plus, with the advent of the Jet Age, the dry lakes of California were being annexed by the federal government to the large air bases, such as Edwards Air Force Base. The dry lake scene was "drying up," and the sport found a willing home in Utah. The racers liked the venue, and the growing performance

The NHRA Safety Caravan and Safari gang had several cool rides, including a pickup, travel trailer, and this trick '59 Chevy Biscayne panel wagon. Kneeling Safety Caravaner is NHRA director Ed Eaton. The Caravan maintained high visibility at all NHRA drag meets and other speed events, emphasizing that speed and safety could work hand in hand. It was revolutionary at the time; in the early days, hot rodding didn't enjoy the best reputation with the public. *Petersen Photo Archive/TEN: The Enthusiast Network*

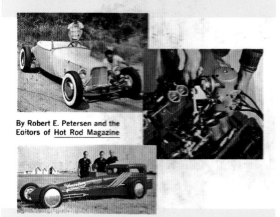

THE COMPLETE BOOK OF HOT RODDING

By Robert E. Petersen and the
Editors of Hot Rod Magazine

For beginners and seasoned hot rodders — the most authoritative material ever compiled on
America's fastest growing sport — from basic theory to latest techniques

* GETTING MORE HORSEPOWER AND TORQUE
FROM YOUR ENGINE * COMPRESSION RATIOS, FUELS, AND FUEL INJECTION * SUPERCHARGING FOR IN-
CREASED PERFORMANCE * CHOOSING THE RIGHT TRANSMISSION * BUILDING YOUR OWN HOT ROD * THE
ABC's OF TROUBLE SHOOTING * ENGINE SWAPPING FOR MORE POWER * VALVES, CARBURETION AND IGNITION
SYSTEMS * ELECTRICAL SYSTEMS * RACING TIRE PROBLEMS

aftermarket industry began sponsoring and supporting Bonneville, while developing more "go-fast" hardware for this now more legit brand of motor racing.

Land-speed-record racing was first held at Bonneville in 1914, but the modern era of salt flats racing began there in 1949—not long after the birth of *Hot Rod*. It should come as no surprise that Petersen and Parks were influential in convincing Utah's governor and the newly formed Bureau of Land Management to allow and support this activity. Some of history's most memorable land-speed records were set at Bonneville.

From its earliest days, hot rodding was seen by many as somewhat of an outlaw sport—not entirely without justification. In many instances, it involved a group of (mostly) young guys who wanted to home-build faster cars, often with the intent of racing each other to see whose ride was king. Some of this activity took place in the relative safety of the dry lakes, but many impromptu speed contests happened on public roads either in semideveloped areas

ABOVE: This charming ad for *Hot Rod* ran in 1954, posing and answering a variety of "how-to" questions. *Author collection*

LEFT: Mr. Petersen considered himself a photographer first, but of course he didn't hesitate to sit down at his typewriter and crank out copy. In this case, it was his first book, *The Complete Book of Hot Rodding*, by "Robert E. Petersen and the editors of *Hot Rod* magazine," published in 1959 and reprinted several times. Now long out of print, it's charming and informative on a variety of technical, philosophical, and artistic subjects related to hot rodding, the cars, and the sport. *Author collection*

outside of towns or even on busy, crowded boulevards. A group of hot rodders would meet up in a parking lot of the local diner, burger joint, or bowling alley, then begin pairing off against the competition. The pack tended to move to less-traveled roads in order to avoid attention from local law enforcement, but more often the cars just lined up at an intersection and waited for the green light, the drop of a scarf, or the signal from a flashlight. Local citizens disdained this "thuggish" pastime, and too many people (participants and bystanders) were hurt or killed.

Petersen and Parks felt that *Hot Rod* could change this game for the better. In 1951, they formed the National Hot Rod Association (NHRA) to establish some standards for accelerative drag racing. The idea was to get drag racing off the streets and into proper venues where crowds and safety issues could be managed; standard rules and practices could

That's R. E. P. wearing the *Hot Rod* staff shirt, swinging his big Speed Graphic press camera at a Bonneville trophy presentation; year unknown. *Petersen Foundation collection*

professionalize the competition with better-defined classes, legitimate timing, and approved scoring protocols. Parks took the role of founder and first president of the new NHRA with the full support of Petersen Publishing Company and *Hot Rod*. NHRA's first "Nationals" event was held in 1955, in Great Bend, Kansas. Typical for the time, it took place at a World War II military air field. The birth of the NHRA also established 1,320 feet—one quarter of a mile—as the standard length for a drag strip (not including an acceptable runoff area immediately after the timing lights), the track used for this form of competition.

ABOVE: Trend/Petersen Publishing may or may not have invented it, but they certainly invested in mining the company's stock of published articles and photographs for "yearbooks, annuals, and special" publications. It was a great way to pull a little extra profit out of material already generated and completed (usually with a few new pieces thrown into the mix), packaging it up topically and releasing a special edition like "Custom Cars, Fastest Cars." This is the yearbook offering for 1956. *Author collection*

RIGHT: Boys will be boys: that's a smiling R. E. P. on the left, with an unidentified pal also aboard a bike at right, out knocking around at someone's garage; the company panel truck is at right. *Petersen Foundation collection*

Parks, Petersen, and the NHRA's members also wanted to reform drag racing's reputation as an illicit activity. The group made a considerable effort, involving all manner of law enforcement in setting up rules and planning events. According to the NHRA:

The original "Drag Safari" [traveling road show touting the NHRA's message] began their tour across America in 1954. Included were four original members: Bud Coons, Bud Evans, [Petersen staffer] Eric Rickman and Chic Cannon. Within the safety requirements, there is also a full crew of safety personnel, called the Safety Safari, *whose job is to attend to any fires, clean up the track of debris after an accident on the track, and attend to the drivers prior to the arrival of any medical personnel. The Safety Safari has been in place since the late 1960s.*

PETERSEN PUBLISHING COMPANY
ANNUAL SALES MEETING
1959
of the advertising staff held april 18 through 25 los angeles, california

Mr. Petersen always insisted that his sales staff look sharp, hence lots of coats and ties from this group roundup of the sales team at PPC's annual sales meetings in 1959. A group that definitely worked hard and is rumored to have played hard too. *Petersen Photo Archive/ TEN, The Enthusiast Network*

A lot had happened in the short period from *Hot Rod*'s humble beginnings in 1947: the birth of the NHRA and SCTA Bonneville racing; the formation of Petersen Publishing Company; and PPC's growth from a single-title publisher to a special interest publishing house commanding the attention of millions of readers by the end of the 1950s. *Hot Rod* alone achieved circulation of half a million by the middle of 1952.

But fasten your seatbelts: New Year's Eve 1959 heralded many great new cars, faster and faster racing, more magazine titles, and the birth of the Detroit muscle car era.

GROUNDBREAKING EVENTS

As far back as 1948, Mr. Petersen had demonstrated that he had a knack for organizing and promoting automotive events, particularly shows focused on hot rodding. The original Hot Rod Exposition ran from 1948–1950, and it wasn't long before Petersen was on his way with a new show, an expanded vision, and a grander location than the Old Armory Building in downtown Los Angeles. The new event was named Motorama (which must have appealed a lot to Mr. P., as it became the name of his first auto museum in the 1970s). The location was the famous, now-demolished Pan-Pacific Auditorium in L.A.'s Fairfax District. The Pan-Pacific was a purpose-built event center with attractive art deco architecture and massive interior spaces. Over time, it hosted Elvis Presley and future Presidents Eisenhower and Nixon, and it was a much larger

Welcome to
Third Annual
International
Motorama

R. E. PETERSEN
Show Producer

LEE. O. RYAN
Managing Director

FOR THE THIRD consecutive year, Motorama, Inc. is pleased and privileged to present to the residents of Southern California this popular and colorful display of motorized equipment.

As soon as the doors had closed on the 1951 show—an unprecedented success—plans for the Third Annual International MOTORAMA were begun. You see here in this Auditorium the results of a year of work and planning.

We have employed the term "International" because MOTORAMA is now truly international in scope. The ever-growing interest in cars and motorcycles from foreign nations and the desire of American motoring enthusiasts to compare these products with our own domestic output is the chief reason for such a representative foreign exhibit on the show floor.

The avid interest of Southern Californians in the progress of motordom is not limited, however, to imports from abroad. It manifests itself in custom cars, in Fiberglas developments, in technical innovations; in fact in almost every facet of the motoring world.

Evidence of this growth of interest can be found in the circulation figures of such publications as *Motor Trend*, *Hot Rod*, *Auto* and *Cycle*, which have experienced phenomenal circulation rises in the past year.

So extraordinary is the revived interest of Americans in things automotive, that several national publications have recently devoted long feature articles to this phenomenon.

In MOTORAMA, we make no attempt to exhibit American stock production cars, believing that these may be seen at any time in dealers' show windows and that they therefore possess no particular show value in an exhibit of this type.

It is, rather, our desire to display those specimens of motorized equipment which are unique or novel or which, for some other special reason, capture the imagination and the fancy of enthusiasts.

Each exhibit on the show floor has been most carefully selected and close scrutiny will show why the selection was made.

This show would not be possible without the complete cooperation of the various owners of cars, motorcycles and other equipment who so graciously have consented to the use of their vehicles for display purposes. Likewise, the various Clubs and Associations have contributed generously to the over-all presentation.

The management of MOTORAMA bids you welcome and trusts that you will find this exposition interesting, fascinating, diverting and educational.

PLEASE
The exhibits which are on display in this show represent something over one million dollars in personal investment. We respectfully request, therefore, that spectators not handle the exhibits. Your cooperation will be greatly appreciated.
The Management

ABOVE: A 1952 Motorama welcome letter from Managing Director Lee Ryan and Robert E. Petersen. *Petersen Foundation collection*

LEFT: Back cover of the Motorama program highlighting a host of Trend Books' popular "Little Pages" titles, each of which sold for only seventy-five cents a copy. *Petersen Foundation collection*

OPPOSITE: This program cover for the Third Annual Motorama event in 1952 illustrates the diversity and variety of cars that attendees could find in the halls of the Pan-Pacific Auditorium in Los Angeles. These were great happenings, focused on race cars, foreign cars produced outside of the US, and, of course, hot rods and customs. *Petersen Foundation collection*

PRICE 25 cents

INTERNATIONAL

MOTORAMA

PAN PACIFIC AUDITORIUM

NOVEMBER 10-16, 1952

CITY OF BURBANK

61 B

From left, longtime Petersen Publishing executive Dick Day, Robert E. Petersen, and Wally Parks at the 1982 SEMA show accepting a special award presented to Petersen Publishing "in grateful recognition for your major contributions to the success of the specialty performance Industry." *Petersen Foundation Collection*

and more prestigious location than the armory. The new International Motorama Show was first staged in 1950 by managing director and local businessman (and soon Petersen Publishing Company senior manager) Lee O. Ryan, with Robert E. Petersen serving as show promoter.

In their welcome letter for the third event in 1952, the pair emphasized the international nature of the show, saying:

> The ever-growing interest in cars and motorcycles from foreign nations and the desire of American motoring enthusiasts to compare these products with our own domestic output is the chief reason for such a representative foreign exhibit on the show floor . . . . Evidence of this growth of interest can be found in the circulation figures of publications such as *Motor Trend, Hot Rod, Auto,* and *Cycle* [all Petersen Publishing titles], which have experienced phenomenal circulation rises in the past year.

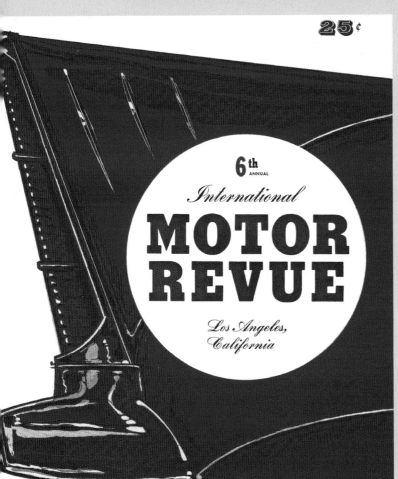

25 ¢

6th ANNUAL

International

MOTOR REVUE

*Los Angeles,
California*

ABOVE: This vintage Eric Rickman shot shows the Trend Inc. booth at one of the Motorama shows, featuring a handsome "track-nosed" hot rod on the left and a mid-engined Bonneville record holder (at over 178 miles per hour) at right, billed as the "World's Fastest Roadster." The sign behind the table offers *Motor Trend* magazine for a dollar per copy. *Petersen Photo Archive/TEN: The Enthusiast Network*

LEFT: Petersen and Ryan really upped their game when their annual car show became the *Motor Revue*. This is the cover of the 1955 event, featuring a stylized illustration of what appears to be a Plymouth tailfin. *Petersen Foundation collection*

UTAH'S SALT FLATS have been called the new proving ground for America's power and speed enthusiasts. In this year's Motor Revue and on these pages there are several examples of the type of equipment that's assaulting the world's speed records on the barren expanses of flat surface. This year no less than 15 records were broken at Bonneville, 12 of them attesting to the superiority of the hemispherical combustion chamber. There's a lot to the story of Bonneville and the engineering going on in the backyards and small speed and equipment shops of these particular brand of enthusiasts; we can't possibly do it justice in this program. Our suggestion: Read the exciting account of this year's event in the November issue of Hot Rod Magazine.

Built from surplus airplane wing tank, Tom Beatty's "C" class Lakester holds 2-way record run at 211.267 mph. Has rear-mounted Mercury engine with GMC blower.

This "D" class competition coupe is basically a '34 Ford, chopped and channeled. Powered by a Chrysler engine, it turned 188.58 mph at recent Bonneville meet.

Jado Special is equipped with Chrysler engine with 180-degree Nordun crank, magnesium rods. Did 175.01 mph. Owner: Jim Kamboor, Sherman Oaks, Calif.

Equipped with an Ardun Merc powerplant, this '53 Studebaker hardtop holds B-class record of 152.935 and C-class record of 155.458 mph. Owners: Sanchez—Cagle—Le Mnon.

Ross-Jacobsen's "D" class modified roadster has a Chrysler V8 with Hilborn fuel injection system. Its 1-way record is 199.66 mph. Ford suspension is used.

The pair added:

In MOTORAMA, we make no attempt to exhibit American stock production cars believing that these may be seen at any time in dealers show windows . . . . It is, rather, our desire to display those specimens of motorized equipment which are unique or novel or which, for some other special reason, capture the imagination and the fancy of enthusiasts.

Hot rods and race cars were still welcome, along with those "funny furrin machines." The event went on to eclipse the Hot Rod Expo.

For 1955, the Motorama event was renamed the Motor Revue Show. In terms of staging and quality of presentation, Motor Revue resembled a major international auto show. But the only American cars on hand were either very limited production makes and models or hot rods and customs. These shows were very well attended and continued for some years, until the expansion of what would become the Los Angeles International Auto Show.

In 1960, Petersen recognized the need for the performance industry to gather, meet, organize, and

ABOVE: The masthead of the Motor Revue program includes the names of many Petersen staffers and editors of the day, with a photo of Petersen, Parks, and Ryan in Mr. Petersen's office. *Petersen Foundation collection*

LEFT: This great page from the Motor Revue program illustrates the depth and variety of cars that competed at Bonneville, from stock hot rods and production cars to streamliners and "belly tankers." *Petersen Foundation collection*

show off its growth and capability, so he developed and founded the Hot Rod Industry Trade Show (HRITS). The first such event was held late that year at Dodger Stadium, with ninety-nine booths presented by seventy-two exhibitors. A few years later, the Specialty Equipment Market Association (SEMA) was formed, and it adopted the HRITS as its own. The show ultimately became the world-famous SEMA industry trade show, now held in Las Vegas each fall; this show is one of the largest industry-only trade shows and conventions in the world. Petersen became an active member of the organization. He was named its Man of the Year in 1972 and inducted into the SEMA Hall of Fame in 1981.

ABOVE: With more elaborate staging than previously seen at the Hot Rod Expo or Motorama, Motor Revue more resembled an international new car auto salon. *Petersen Foundation collection*

LEFT: This "house ad" highlighted *Motor Trend*, *Hot Rod*, *Rod & Custom*, *Motor Life*, and *Car Craft* as the "Trend family of magazines." *Petersen Foundation collection*

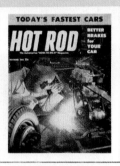

WELCOME TO MOTOR REVUE FROM THE TREND FAMILY

HOT ROD

The *Automotive HOW-TO-DO-IT* magazine. The favorite of HOT ROD fans, for all mechanics, and everyone who tinkers with cars. How to build Hot Rods, custom cars for performance and individuality; facts on new engines. The latest and most authentic in Hot Rod activities.

MOTOR TREND

The *CAR OWNERS* magazine. The favorite for all car owners with unbiased road test reports on all stock cars, trends in design, custom and sports cars. The fact-packed magazine about all cars the world over.

ROD & CUSTOM

First in coverage of the custom world. Brings you the latest in Hot Rods and all types of "HOW TO DO ITS". Here you can follow the leadership of such automotive experts as: Roger Huntington, John Christy, Lynn Wineland, and many others.

CAR CRAFT

The *SHOW HOW* magazine that is a favorite with the "do it yourself" auto expert. Tops in the customizing field with step-by-step instructions, graphically illustrated; on restyling and remodeling.

On sale at your newsstands now!

MOTOR LIFE

The favorite magazine for motoring for reports on WHAT'S NEW and WHAT'S COMING in the automotive world. Latest in styling, engines, accessories. Tops in road testing.

The Swinging '60s and the Hot Rod King Finds a Queen

Petersen Publishing hit the new decade at full stride, with a growing and capable staff of editors, writers, ad sales people, and photographers, along with its increasing roster of titles. Fortunately, there was a lot to talk about, largely driven by the formalization and growth of motorsports. There was

plenty of go-fast news to report on: beyond the organization of land-speed-record racing (Bonneville and such), drag racing continued to mature, and February 1948 saw the birth of NASCAR, just a month after publication of *Hot Rod's* first issue.

At this point, none of Petersen's titles was exclusively dedicated to racing. Speed required performance, though, which meant that fast cars—or the parts and technology that made them that way—were important features for the avid readers. Remember that the NHRA was born in the offices of *Hot Rod* and run by *Hot Rod's* editor Parks; hot rodding cut its proverbial teeth on the dry lakes and the salt flats, so those scenes were elemental to each enthusiast movement.

There were many changes that Petersen, *Hot Rod*, and PPC witnessed, covered, and, in many cases, took part in during the 1960s.

OPPOSITE: "TV Tommy" Ivo and his Buick Nailhead V-8 x 4 powered show dragster not only made a frightfully loud noise ripping through the quarter miles, but due to its all-wheel drive, could burn rubber for 1,000 feet with no problem, yet tons of smoke. Eric Rickman bagged this December 1961 cover shot, and the headlines (see cover on page 78) covering tech stories, photo features, a new engine from Buick, and Bonneville were typical of the era. *Petersen Photo Archive/TEN: The Enthusiast Network*

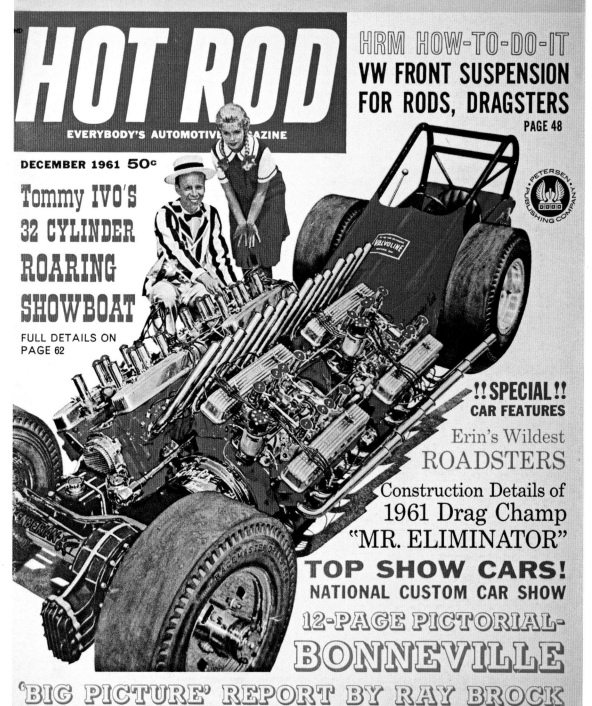

BUICK'S ALL-NEW V6

TECH REPORT: by R. Huntington

HOT ROD

EVERYBODY'S AUTOMOTIVE MAGAZINE

HRM HOW-TO-DO-IT
VW FRONT SUSPENSION FOR RODS, DRAGSTERS
PAGE 48

DECEMBER 1961 50¢

Tommy IVO'S 32 CYLINDER ROARING SHOWBOAT

FULL DETAILS ON PAGE 62

PETERSEN PUBLISHING COMPANY

!!SPECIAL!!
CAR FEATURES

Erin's Wildest
ROADSTERS

Construction Details of
1961 Drag Champ
"MR. ELIMINATOR"

TOP SHOW CARS!
NATIONAL CUSTOM CAR SHOW

12-PAGE PICTORIAL—
BONNEVILLE

'BIG PICTURE' REPORT BY RAY BROCK

LEFT: Petersen and Parks hash out cover designs and photo layouts in front of the now much-expanded PPC roster of magazine titles. Even though Parks was technically the editor of *Hot Rod*, he also wore an editorial director title and contributed to other PPC titles. R. E. P. is pointing to one of PPC's best-ever titles, *Sports Car Graphic*, which was, as you might guess, focused on sports cars and road racing. Several of its editors were racing writers who raced cars competitively and then wrote of their experiences. *Petersen Photo Archive/TEN: The Enthusiast Network*

BELOW: *Hot Rod*'s first official editor Wally Parks departed in 1962. *Petersen Photo Archive/TEN: The Enthusiast Network*

One of the most foundational was Wally Parks's departure from *Hot Rod* in 1962 to take over the now full-time job of running the NHRA. Drag racing was maturing into a big-time professional sport (and business), so it needed its leader fully on the case. This was a sea change in continuity for the magazine, but all things evolve, and *Hot Rod* evolved with the times.

There are many opinions about where the Detroit factory muscle car movement really began. Signs of post–World War II interest in performance cars were clearly evident beginning in the 1950s. But some would say it first manifested itself with new developments in overhead valve engine design, such as the Oldsmobile Rocket 88 V-8 of 1949 and Cadillac's fabulous new overhead valver that same year; these engines breathed better and revved higher than all the old flathead designs of the prewar era.

Mission accomplished. In the photo at right, the 5959 Hollywood Boulevard office building sports the Trend Inc. sign; this photo was likely taken around 1957, as that's the unmistakable fin of a '57 Chevy Bel Air in the lower right foreground. By the 1963 photo below, "5959" had been the home of Petersen Publishing Company for some years—now, without question, it was "the house that Pete built." *Petersen Photo Archive/TEN: The Enthusiast Network*

Lincoln introduced its own all-new engine architecture in 1952, and Ford and Mercury followed along with similar, but not identical, "Y-block" V-8s in 1954; these replaced Ford's venerable, veteran flathead V-8 that had served so ably since 1932. Ford developed a dual four-barrel carbed version of this engine for the two-seat Thunderbird in 1956, followed up by an optional supercharged T-Bird for 1957. Chevrolet introduced its world-changing small-block V-8 for 1955 and almost immediately began offering hotter Power Pack versions of it.

Some make a case that the first application of installing a large engine into a midsize car was the 1956 Studebaker Golden Hawk, which ran a powerful 352-cubic-inch Packard V-8 good for 275 horsepower. Another, more obscure, example of this philosophy was the 1957–1960 Rambler Rebel, a somewhat prosaic-looking midsize economy sedan packed with American Motors' new 327-cubic-inch V-8, believed to be conservatively rated at 255 horsepower. A fuel-injected model introduced as an option on the 1957 Rambler Rebel, with an eye toward racing at Daytona, was said to be good for 288 horsepower.

The seminal definition of the modern American muscle car crystallized when a small group of Pontiac engineers, executives, and advertising account reps stuffed a 389-cubic-inch V-8 into the midsize Pontiac Tempest, creating the 1964 Pontiac GTO. This set off a tidal wave of new powermongers from the rest of GM's divisions, as well as from every other American carmaker that offered midsize models.

And *Hot Rod* covered them all.

Evidence that *Hot Rod* was on the case of factory performance developments is clearly *continued on page 90*

"Melding the new with the traditional" describes this March 1957 *Hot Rod* cover, which shows off Studebaker's lush and fast Golden Hawk coupe, as well as a properly hot-rodded Flathead V-8 and a tech piece on how to swap a Chevy small-block V-8 into your sports car. *Petersen Photo Archive/TEN: The Enthusiast Network*

Every magazine company dedicated to automotive performance needs a racetrack nearby, for races to cover, events to hold, and for a place to safely test cars and performance claims. Mr. Petersen is second from left, with Ray Brock next to him leaning on the humble "hut" at the start/finish line of the new Riverside International Raceway (RIR). The man on the right, on the phone, is Les Richter, RIR's leader for nineteen years. *Petersen Photo Archive/TEN: The Enthusiast Network*

THE WRITER AND THE RACE QUEEN

Gigi Carleton tells the story . . .

"Mr. Petersen was quite the ladies' man in the '50s and early '60s as he was handsome, young, and had become a multimillionaire because of his publishing empire. So he was a real catch for Hollywood actresses and other local young ladies.

"He dated many starlets, knew Howard Hughes, and double-dated with Mr. Hughes back in the '50s. One evening in Hollywood at a large party, he saw a friend of his enter with a beautiful lady on each arm. One of these stunning young women was dazzling, flame-haired fashion model Margie McNally, from New York. Mr. P. made it his business to meet Margie and chat with her for a few minutes, but that's as far as it went at that time. Mr. P. had a sales office in New York and often visited The City to meet clients. He was immediately taken with the petite redhead, 5 feet 5 inches tall, with her natural peaches-and-cream complexion, tiny waist, perfect skin, electric smile, and warm brown eyes. Later in 1961 or possibly 1962, he asked his

BELOW: R. E. P. and the future Mrs. Petersen pose up on the hood of a Stroppe Mercury stocker driven by Troy Ruttman in the race. *Petersen Photo Archive/TEN: The Enthusiast Network*

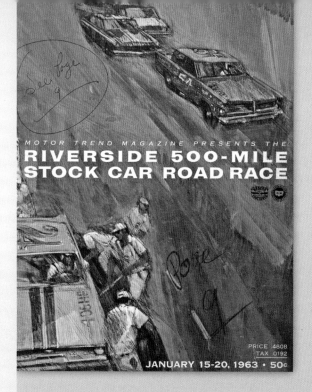

MOTOR TREND MAGAZINE PRESENTS THE

RIVERSIDE 500-MILE STOCK CAR ROAD RACE

PRICE 4808
TAX 0192

JANUARY 15-20, 1963 • 50¢

QUEEN

Selected to reign over the Riverside 500-Mile Stock Car Road Race, Queen Margie McNally is a familiar face on television. You've seen her as Wendell Corey's and Jack Ging's gal Friday in MGM-TV's psychiatric series, "The Eleventh Hour." Until she was signed to an MGM contract, Margie's familiarity with the public rested largely on her career as a vivacious fashion model for dozens of cosmetic, soft drink, cigarette, and swim-suit commercials.

Margie is a five-foot, five-and-a-half-inch, red-head who tips the scales at 110 pounds. She was born June 23 in Queens, New York, the daughter of distinctly Irish parents, Patrick and Margaret McNally. Following graduation from Prospect High School in New York City, Margie was discovered by famed fashion model impresario John Robert Powers in 1953, who spied her as the winner of the "Candy Queen" high school beauty contest. She modeled for him until 1958, and soon gained the reputation as the "All American" type in magazines not only throughout the U.S. but Europe as well. In 1960 she went to Paris where she worked as a much-in-demand model for many French magazines. Margie considered herself fortunate to work for such houses as Dior and Givenchy. Before coming to MGM, the brown-eyed actress spent some time modeling in Nassau, Bermuda, and the Dutch West Indies. Her first American TV commercial, for Coca Cola, was done in 1955 on the Eddie Fisher weekly network show. In 1961 Margie gave up a lucrative modeling career for straight drama. Following a number of choice roles on Kraft and Philco Playhouse, "Danger," as well as hostessing assignments on the "Today" and "Home" shows, she won a regular co-starring spot on "The Charlie Weaver Show." When she's not before the movie or still cameras at MGM, Margie totes her shotgun off to a local range and bones up on her skeet and trap shooting, swims, or goes deep sea fishing on friends' boats. "Just sitting down and talking to people on any subject is also a great way of putting my spare time to good advantage," she says.

ABOVE LEFT: At the time, NASCAR only competed on road courses twice a year: at Watkins Glen, New York, and at the Riverside International Raceway. It was a momentous time for Mr. Petersen and race queen Margie McNally: they staged the *Motor Trend* 500, then got married the following week. *Petersen Foundation collection*

ABOVE RIGHT: Queen, indeed. The petite and wholesome yet minxy Margie McNally, before she became Mrs. Margie Petersen. Here she's featured in the program for the 1963 *Motor Trend* 500 NASCAR race held at Riverside. *Petersen Foundation collection*

friend if it would be okay to call Margie when he was next in New York. His friend said yes and gave Mr. P. Margie's phone number.

"Their friend in common called Margie and let her know that he had given her phone number to Mr. P., who would probably call her the next time he was in New York. Of course he called Margie, who shared an apartment with three other top New York models that weren't using the apartment at the time and she had a preexisting date with a gentleman who had showered her with flowers—so much so, Mrs. P. recalled that 'the place looked like a funeral home.' After talking with Mr. P., who asked her out for dinner that same night, she called the other gentleman friend and cancelled their date.

"Mr. P. was great friends with the often rough-talking Texan Carroll Shelby, who also happened to be in New York at the time. Mr. P. had arranged for a double date with Margie and had invited Carroll and a friend to join them. Mr. P. told Carroll to watch his language 'because I like this girl' and to be a gentleman since Margie was the girl he was going to marry.

"Their first date was at a very romantic restaurant named Chez Vito on the Upper East Side of New York featuring live violinists performing tableside. Mr. P. proposed to Margie that evening—on their first date! I am not sure if she really believed him in the moment but always said that he proposed to her that way.

"Time went by and Mr. P. made ever-more-frequent trips to New York than usual—surprise, surprise. In the meantime, Margie got a call from MGM Studios—yes, by this time she'd also begun making a name for herself as an actress—who wanted to sign her as a contract player. Incidentally, Linda Evans of *Dallas* TV fame and Margie were the last actresses to be signed by MGM. Bear in mind that Margie was definitely an East Coast New York gal, a top fashion model [who had also worked extensively in Paris], up-and-coming actress, and regular line dancer and singer on television for *The Eddie Fisher Show* and *The Jack Carter Show*, and had traveled Europe on a variety of fantastic modeling assignments. Without hesitation and ignoring her agent and lawyer's advice, she accepted the offer from MGM so she could come

BELOW: Race queen Margie McNally smiles as she guards the purse paid out to the winners of the *Motor Trend* 500. Dan Gurney took home a fair share of those hundred-dollar bills. *Petersen Photo Archive/TEN: The Enthusiast Network*

FOLLOWING PAGES: This is the 1965 *Motor Trend* 500 Pace Car Pontiac GTO, specially modified and painted in the famous Hurst Golden Shifter Girls livery, with George Hurst standing left in the passenger compartment and R. E. P. at right. *Petersen Photo Archive/ TEN: The Enthusiast Network*

JANUARY 20, 1963
Riverside "500" Stock Car Race
PURSE $66,245.00

EY DISPLAYED COURTESY MANUFACTURERS BANK

PACE CAR · MOTOR TREND RIVERSIDE "500"
EQUIPPED & AWARDED BY
HURST

The publishing king and his future queen take parade laps aboard the new Mercury Monterey S-55 pace car convertible before the start of the 1963 MT500 at Riverside. Note the "VIP Grandstand" just behind the car, consisting of a row of chairs assembled on the flat deck of a semi trailer. *Petersen Photo Archive/TEN: The Enthusiast Network*

to Hollywood. She never told Mr. P. what she had given up—a model's potentially large salary—and played a little hard to get. It must have worked since the next thing she knew, they were officially engaged.

"Mr. Petersen, along with nine other partners, including Bob Hope, Ed Pauley, and Bob Estes, had bought and developed the Riverside International Raceway and had begun staging racing events, including the NASCAR *Motor Trend* 500 in January of each year. When Margie and Mr. P. got engaged, she became Miss *Motor Trend* 500 for the next race in January 1963. They set a wedding date of January 26, 1963, just following the NASCAR race. When the discussion of a honeymoon came up, Mr. P. faced a bit of a dilemma. He had long planned a hunting trip in Mexico and asked Margie if she would come along, and then he would take her to Acapulco for a proper romantic honeymoon. And they did just that.

"Little did Margie know that her life as a New York City girl was going to change to that of Hollywood West Coast Girl, including outdoor activities, yachting, and car races. But she truly loved Mr. P. and wanted to be part of his life, and she made the big adjustment and never regretted it. All through the years, Mr. P. always invited Mrs. P. to every business trip, hunting trip, and safari he went on, or to attend every race, wherever it was. Today we'd say that Margie McNally Petersen, who in spite of giving up her career as what we now call a 'supermodel' for love, really had game."

ABOVE: The newly minted Mr. and Mrs. Robert E. Petersen, driven by best man Herb Shriner in PPC classic car editor Robert J. Gottlieb's Rolls-Royce town car to and from their wedding and reception. Throughout their legendary lives, they were a stunning couple. *Petersen Foundation collection*

LEFT: Petersen and All American Racer Dan Gurney share some victory champagne; the trophy girl at left is unidentified. Gurney became known as the "King of Riverside" by winning the MT500 NASCAR race there a record five times. *Petersen Photo Archive/TEN: The Enthusiast Network*

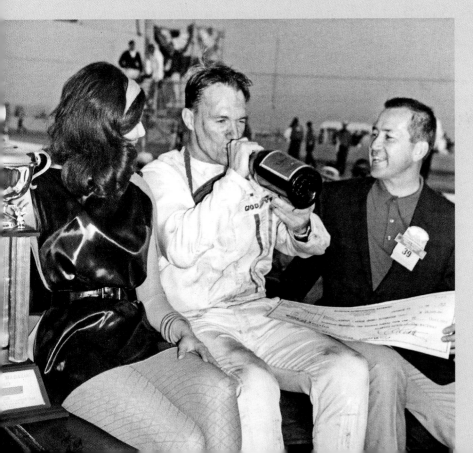

ABOVE: We can't tell who looked more uncomfortable in this posed "corporate-style" photo, Mr. Petersen at left or GM executive John Z. DeLorean, right. The pair was together for an awards presentation when the Pontiac Division won *Motor Trend*'s Car of the Year Awards in 1965. *Petersen Photo Archive/TEN: The Enthusiast Network*

OPPOSITE: *Hot Rod* magazine was sold from pop-up newsstands and card tables at the races from the very beginning. You could still buy a copy that way as late as this 1964 photo; the vendor is unidentified. *Petersen Photo Archive/TEN: The Enthusiast Network*

continued from page 81

demonstrated by a look at the 1957 covers. January's cover heralded a test of the '57 Ford Fairlane 500 and showed stock and custom Chevrolets. The February cover bragged of a test of the new Olds 88, and March featured the Studebaker Golden Hawk. June's cover posed the question: "Pontiac—1957's hottest?" The July cover promoted a test of the new for 1957 Ford Ranchero and also featured new Mercury and Plymouth models. And the innovations kept appearing in issue after issue.

Was *Hot Rod* becoming *Motor Trend*? Not at all, but as carmakers developed ever-more-powerful and hotter hardware, available as close as your new car dealership, *Hot Rod* was going to keep up with the fast-moving performance scene, no matter if it was homegrown or factory built.

Not every reader was happy with *Hot Rod* following this tack, so the editors also kept the pages filled with a steady diet of engine swaps, hop-up articles, drag racing, and the happenings at the salt flats. Coverage of Detroit-built performance proved a wise choice, as this expanded editorial vision opened up the magazine to new readers, and also to a greater variety of advertisers. Carmakers saw that *Hot Rod* was speaking more directly to their car-buying customers, covering their products, stock car racing, and the stock drag racing classes; they in turn began advertising their hottest models in *Hot Rod*. Even when *Hot Rod* ran an article about a "boring economy car," such as the Ford Falcon, Plymouth Valiant, or Chevrolet Corvair, it featured tips on how to hot-rod the vehicle, race, or make it perform better.

Everybody won.

The early 1960s brought many changes for Petersen: new cars, new titles, new events to produce, a new wife, the ramping up of the new car performance scene, and the maturation and growth of the automotive

aftermarket. The introduction of three new cars was the biggest news of all: the new-for-1963 Chevrolet Corvette Stingray, the Pontiac GTO, and the Ford Mustang. Another trend changed the face of hot rodding and racing of all types: introduced in 1955, the Chevrolet small-block V-8 was already famous for its combination of relatively light weight, toughness, willingness to rev to high rpms, and capacity for increased horsepower.

Now it was replacing the venerable Ford flathead V-8 as the rodders' and racers' engine of choice. The performance aftermarket industry really took to the hot new Chevy engine, quickly developing all manner of high-performance parts and accessories for it.

These changes played into Petersen Publishing's hands in several ways. Hot new cars like the Corvette, GTO, and Mustang demonstrated Detroit's increasing involvement in performance cars—and the racing that went along with them; this created great editorial opportunities for publishers like Petersen. In addition, those faster factory cars and the increased selection of speed parts from the growing aftermarket created advertising demand for PPC.

As *Hot Rod* and the rest of the Petersen editorial fleet continued to grow, it attracted more talented writers. While it would take an immense family tree to chart them all, one significant addition was Eric Dahlquist. Eric grew up a member of Buffalo, New York's active hot rodding scene. While attending the University of Buffalo in the late 1950s and early 1960s, he helped pay for college by serving as a freelance stringer for *Hot Rod*, covering drag racing and car builders throughout western New York. After graduating from the university with a degree in history, he was hired by *Hot Rod* as a staff writer and moved to Los Angeles in 1964. Veteran *Hot Rod* staffers taught him the ropes of magazine publishing, and he soon became the magazine's technical editor. Dahlquist was known for several groundbreaking stories of the day, one being the first major article and drag racing test of Chrysler's then-new, all-conquering 426-cubic-inch "Street Hemi" V-8 in 1964. Just three years later, he participated in the creation and production of an important Ford Mustang muscle car.

Petersen Publishing veteran editor Drew Hardin tells the story:

More often than not, when I pull up road tests from the mid-1960s, the guy whose shoes I fantasize about walking in is Eric Dahlquist, Hot Rod *magazine's tech editor and, later, the editor of* Motor Trend. *Dahlquist passed away in December 2016, one more loss in a year that saw too many of them. He worked at Petersen Publishing*

OPPOSITE: Being editor of *Motor Trend* was a bit of a glam position at times. Editor in Chief Eric Dahlquist mugs with actor/racer James Garner with the 1979 Pontiac "Trans-Am sport wagon" concept car, foreground, and one of Garner's Rockford Files Firebird Esprits background. *Author collection*

from 1964 to 1975, absolute prime time for the rise (and fall) of Detroit muscle. It was Dahlquist who tested the first Street Hemi for Hot Rod, *and also the first new Camaro. Maybe most famously, it was his article in the Nov. 1967* Hot Rod *about [Ford dealer] Bob Tasca's KR-8 performance package for the 1968 Mustang, and his encouraging readers to write directly to Henry Ford II about it, [all of] which resulted in Ford building the 1968½ Mustang Cobra Jet.*

Dahlquist transferred to *Motor Trend* in 1968, ultimately ending up as its editor in chief for many years before leaving Petersen and forming his own media, public relations, and product placement firm called Vista Group. PPC was often a client, and Dahlquist continued his relationship with Petersen Publishing for the rest of his career.

The year 1970 was the absolute zenith of factory performance cars born in the late 1950s and evolved throughout the 1960s. By the turn of the decade, the engines were larger, compression ratios were higher, and horsepower was king. But times were changing, and the factory performance tide was turning. Several factors conspired, including the birth of the Environmental Protection Agency (EPA) and the subsequent Clean Air Act of 1968. At the same time, the insurance industry was concerned about carmakers selling what were ostensibly factory-built race cars to anyone who could walk into a dealership and fork over an easy down payment. The government and public alike were becoming ever more concerned with automotive safety.

As the 1970s approached, then, large-displacement, high-compression, big-horsepower engines were on their way out, along with leaded gasoline. All of a sudden, safety, fuel mileage, emissions, and similar issues were more important to many people than big, smoky, tire-melting burnouts, 0–60 times, and top speed. Suddenly, headrests, seat belts, fuel mileage, and bumper regulations beat out horsepower as the stories of the day.

What were hot rodders—and *Hot Rod*—to do?

OPPOSITE: Hold on a minute! Does that Olds 4-4-2 Funny Car really have two engines? It certainly does. Dubbed the Hurst Hairy Olds, this four-wheel-drive exhibition dragster was commissioned by the always promotion-minded George Hurst and driven by Gigi Carleton's husband, "Gentleman Joe" Schubeck, for this memorable "see-through" May 1966 *Hot Rod* cover. *Petersen Photo Archive/TEN: The Enthusiast Network*

CRUISE-O-MATIC FOR DRAGS

MAY 1966 50c

UK 3/6   Sweden KR 3.90 Inkl oms

HOT ROD

EVERYBODY'S AUTOMOTIVE MAGAZINE

**STREET-STRIP TEST
327 CHEVY EL CAMINO**

**TECH TIPS!
BORING & STROKING**

**DRIVING THE HIGH BANKS—
DAYTONA 500**

LANDY'S NEW GAME: DARTS

HAIRY OLDS!!!

HURST'S TWIN ENGINE
4-WHEEL DRIVE
FUEL BURNING
SMOKER

FIRST OF THE 1970 MUSCLE CARS

HOT ROD

EVERYBODY'S AUTOMOTIVE MAGAZINE

"JR. STOCKING" 283 CHEVYS

BRAND-NEW 90-HP 1700 VW

CARTER CARB POWER MODS

BORG-WARNER AUTOMATIC O.

ALL-OUT 340 MOPARS-Part II

EMBER 1969   50¢   UK 4/3   Sweden KR. 3.95 Inkl. moms

ORD TORINO

FORD

COBRA

1970

PLYMOUTH 'CU

HOT
70s

ODGE CHALLENGER

4

Into the '70s, '80s, and Beyond— Petersen People, Places, and Things

J ust as the 1970s muscle car era was peaking, it was being put out of business. Changing times, environmental awareness, and evolving politics offered generally positive growth for society— but not often ways that favored traditional hot rodding. Questions were being asked: how were cars

affecting the quality of air and other natural resources? Could vehicle safety be improved? Motorsports, hot rodding, new carmakers, and the enthusiast press that covered those scenes risked extinction if it didn't evolve.

Beginning around 1968, government-mandated safety and emissions regulations began to have an impact on car design, engineering, and production. By the following year, high-backed seats and headrests, intended to protect against whiplash and other head and neck injuries, became mandatory for any carmaker selling in the United States. Vehicle lighting regulations also changed, with side-marker lights, larger taillights, brighter headlights, and such added to the list of requirements. Ignition switches that had been mounted on a car's dashboard were moved, by law, to lockable steering columns intended to thwart vehicle theft; the ignition key started the car and controlled

OPPOSITE: The absolute zenith of midcentury muscle came in 1970, as the engines were bigger, the compression ratios and horsepower ratings were higher, and the cars were faster than ever before. Just as the original Detroit muscle car era reached its peak, though, it began a precipitous slide down the same mountain. Every car on this September 1969 *Hot Rod* cover is now a highly sought-after model. *Petersen Photo Archive/TEN: The Enthusiast Network*

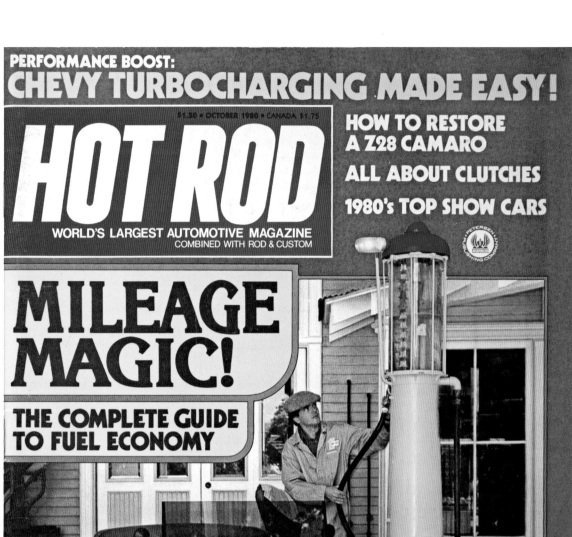

PERFORMANCE BOOST:
CHEVY TURBOCHARGING MADE EASY!

$1.50 • OCTOBER 1980 • CANADA, $1.75

HOT ROD

WORLD'S LARGEST AUTOMOTIVE MAGAZINE
COMBINED WITH ROD & CUSTOM

HOW TO RESTORE A Z28 CAMARO
ALL ABOUT CLUTCHES
1980's TOP SHOW CARS

MILEAGE MAGIC!

THE COMPLETE GUIDE TO FUEL ECONOMY

LEFT: The trend toward building up, hot rodding, and modifying late-model muscle cars became known as the "street machine" movement. This always struck us as a little odd; unless it's a pure racing car run on a racetrack, isn't every car a "street machine"? No matter, it was something to address the changing times. *Petersen Photo Archive/TEN: The Enthusiast Network*

OPPOSITE: Fuel mileage was something most hot rodders didn't much care about until the fuel shortages of the 1970s, and certainly it wasn't a topic written about in the pages of *Hot Rod* until this October 1980 issue. The *Hot Rod* editors did the best with what they had, as they attempted to adjust to the ever-changing times and priorities of government regulations, politics, society, and hot rodders. Reinventing the magazine for this new era—faced with so many complex issues, rising fuel prices, and the declining popularity of speed and performance—wasn't an easy task. *Petersen Photo Archive/TEN: The Enthusiast Network*

the steering wheel column lock. (Most Swedish Saab models, however, kept the ignition switches on the floor console near the shifter.)

Following on the heels of these regulations came a variety of new equipment: catalytic converters, exhaust gas recirculation, and five-mile-an-hour bumpers. Hot rodders hadn't anticipated these additions, nor did they like handling and installing them on their vehicles. Horsepower fell like a popped balloon as the big engines went away; the biggest

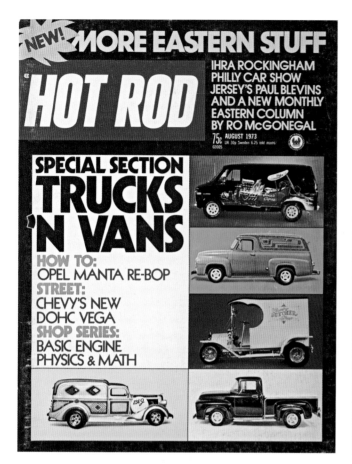

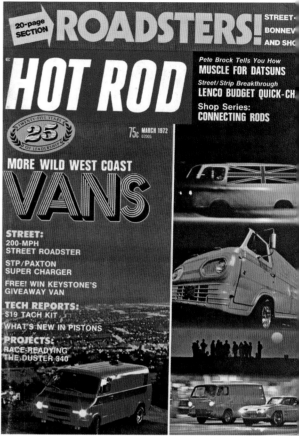

one available in a Corvette in 1976 was 350 cubic inches, and horsepower was down to a piddling 180. When Ford downsized the Mustang into the Mustang II for 1974, it wasn't even offered with a V-8 engine that first year; the hottest engine available was an optional V-6 good for 105 horses. The muscle car era, at least for the time being, was over. Most agree that the last true product of the original 1960s–1970s muscle car era was the Pontiac Trans Am SD (Super Duty) 455 of 1974, prior to the onset of the catalytic converter and the (mostly) single-exhaust era.

Many states initiated smog checks to make sure that factory pollution control equipment installed on cars at the time of manufacture was in fact present, accounted for, and operating. Noise restrictions also curtailed the performance exhaust

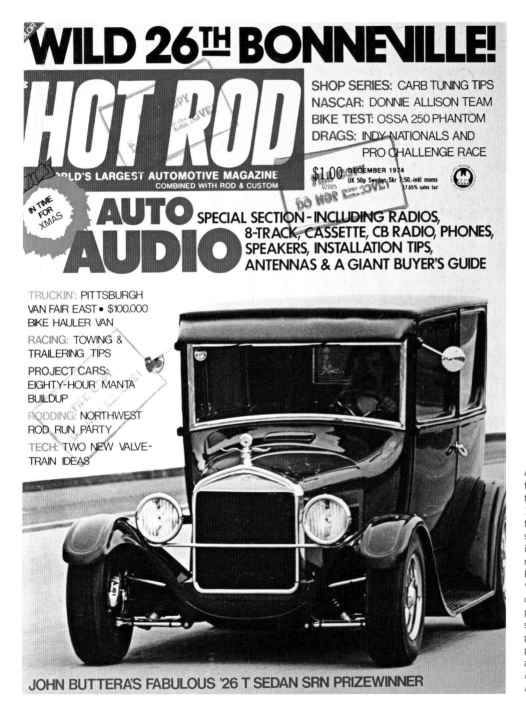

WILD 26TH BONNEVILLE!

HOT ROD
WORLD'S LARGEST AUTOMOTIVE MAGAZINE
COMBINED WITH ROD & CUSTOM

SHOP SERIES: CARB TUNING TIPS
NASCAR: DONNIE ALLISON TEAM
BIKE TEST: OSSA 250 PHANTOM
DRAGS: INDY NATIONALS AND
PRO CHALLENGE RACE

$1.00 DECEMBER 1974
UK 50p Sweden Skr 7.50-inkl moms
17.65% sales tax
02005

IN TIME FOR XMAS

AUTO AUDIO
SPECIAL SECTION - INCLUDING RADIOS, 8-TRACK, CASSETTE, CB RADIO, PHONES, SPEAKERS, INSTALLATION TIPS, ANTENNAS & A GIANT BUYER'S GUIDE

TRUCKIN': PITTSBURGH
VAN FAIR EAST • $100,000
BIKE HAULER VAN

RACING: TOWING &
TRAILERING TIPS

PROJECT CARS:
EIGHTY-HOUR MANTA
BUILDUP

RODDING: NORTHWEST
ROD RUN PARTY

TECH: TWO NEW VALVE-
TRAIN IDEAS

JOHN BUTTERA'S FABULOUS '26 T SEDAN SRN PRIZEWINNER

Another cover feature that really riled up the readers was this 1974 cover dedicated to stereo and audio systems, tech, and installations. Racer, rodder, and car builder Bill Stroppe said, "Well, the government doesn't let you sell performance anymore, so you gotta give the people something!" Not popular, but it worked at the time. *Petersen Photo Archive/TEN: The Enthusiast Network*

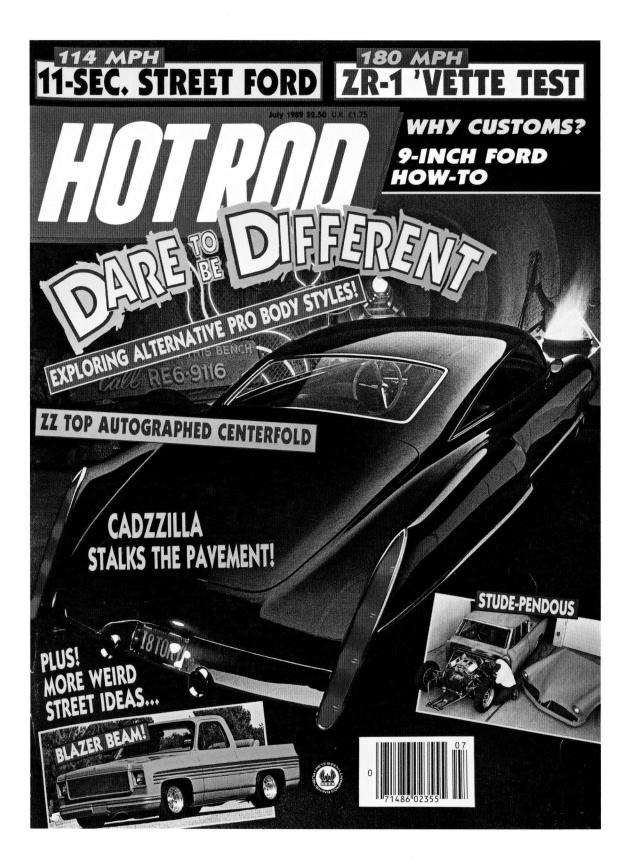

114 MPH
11-SEC. STREET FORD

180 MPH
ZR-1 'VETTE TEST

July 1989 $2.50 U.K. £1.75

HOT ROD

WHY CUSTOMS?
9-INCH FORD HOW-TO

DARE TO BE DIFFERENT

EXPLORING ALTERNATIVE PRO BODY STYLES!

ZZ TOP AUTOGRAPHED CENTERFOLD

CADZZILLA STALKS THE PAVEMENT!

STUDE-PENDOUS

PLUS!
MORE WEIRD
STREET IDEAS...

BLAZER BEAM!

07

0   71486 02355

industry's potential. All this to say that it wasn't easy being a hot rodder, or muscle car enthusiast, in the mid-1970s.

Hot Rod's leadership knew the magazine must adapt to this new normal. SEMA took an active role in organizing its membership to work with the government to establish rules that would allow certain types of aftermarket and performance modifications to be considered legal, and it encouraged performance enthusiasts not to try cheating with, disabling, or removing safety and emissions hardware. This brilliant approach led directly to the performance renaissance that began in the 1980s and continues today, especially with equipment that doesn't violate safety and emissions laws.

In the meantime, *Hot Rod* did the best it could with what was available, embracing the new trends whenever possible. That meant covering and developing more information about the new "emissions era" engines, such as smaller V-8s, V-6s, four-cylinders, and turbocharged engines. It wasn't always easy, and

ABOVE: "Low-buck" building is another innovative *Hot Rod* issue theme, popular when it was coined and still popular today. Who doesn't want to drive a cool car and save a few dollars? Expect this 1987 cover theme to be repeated again every year or two, with a fresh supply of new feature cars to help illustrate the philosophy, theme, and techniques. *Petersen Photo Archive/TEN: The Enthusiast Network*

OPPOSITE: Boyd Coddington's Cadzilla, built for ZZ Top's rocker car guy Billy F. Gibbons, absolutely defined "dare to be different." It's a lavishly designed and beautifully built custom rod, setting the tone for a movement. And it still happens to look fresh and fabulous some three decades after it was built. *Petersen Photo Archive/TEN: The Enthusiast Network*

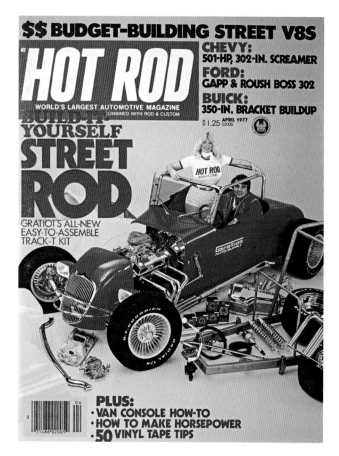

$$ BUDGET-BUILDING STREET V8S

HOT ROD
WORLD'S LARGEST AUTOMOTIVE MAGAZINE
COMBINED WITH ROD & CUSTOM

CHEVY: 501-HP, 302-IN. SCREAMER
FORD: GAPP & ROUSH BOSS 302
BUICK: 350-IN. BRACKET BUILDUP

$1.25 **APRIL 1977** 02005

BUILD-IT YOURSELF STREET ROD

GRATIOT'S ALL-NEW EASY-TO-ASSEMBLE TRACK-T KIT

PLUS:
- VAN CONSOLE HOW-TO
- HOW TO MAKE HORSEPOWER
- 50 VINYL TAPE TIPS

ABOVE: If there was ever a woman who has earned the title of "Perennial Miss *Hot Rod*," it must be the incomparable Linda Vaughn, the supreme ambassadress of motorsport. Linda's fabulous figure, big blonde hair, and glowing persona have made her a worldwide celebrity. She's appeared many times in the pages of *Hot Rod* and other PPC titles. Here she is as Miss Hurst Golden Shifter in 1977. Racers and hot rodders will love her always. *Petersen Photo Archive/TEN: The Enthusiast Network*

OPPOSITE: "Where it all began." July 2004 signaled the rebirth of *Hot Rod* magazine after a long, slow period of somewhat aimless wandering. With this issue, Mr. Petersen called editor David Freiburger to tell him and the *Hot Rod* staff that the magazine was back on track—big stuff from the guy who invented the recipe. *Petersen Photo Archive/TEN: The Enthusiast Network*

it was rarely popular, but following these trends was necessary for the magazine to remain relevant and survive.

The changes also meant running more coverage of older cars and the traditional rodding scene, where all of the new laws and regulations didn't necessarily apply. The *Hot Rod* editors committed more ink and page space to trucks and vans, stereo and audio, interiors, paint, and other topics that wouldn't rankle the Feds or fly in the face of societal and political trends. It wasn't always popular, but it was the hand they were dealt. They made the new focus work, attacking those topics with as much authority and enthusiasm as they did camshafts and carburetors.

Some of the new themes and movements *Hot Rod* hit on during these tough times proved popular and remain so today. Editor Jeff Smith distilled the "Dare to be Different" movement in his pieces, illustrating how many cars and brands, particularly in certain body styles, were becoming more collectible in their restored original condition—and thus more expensive. With this, *Hot Rod* began featuring alternative brands and body styles that had been considered less popular, such as Studebakers, Nashes, Ramblers, even Mercurys and Cadillacs—cars that most performance car builders and hot rodders hadn't traditionally considered viable for their purposes.

continued on page 112

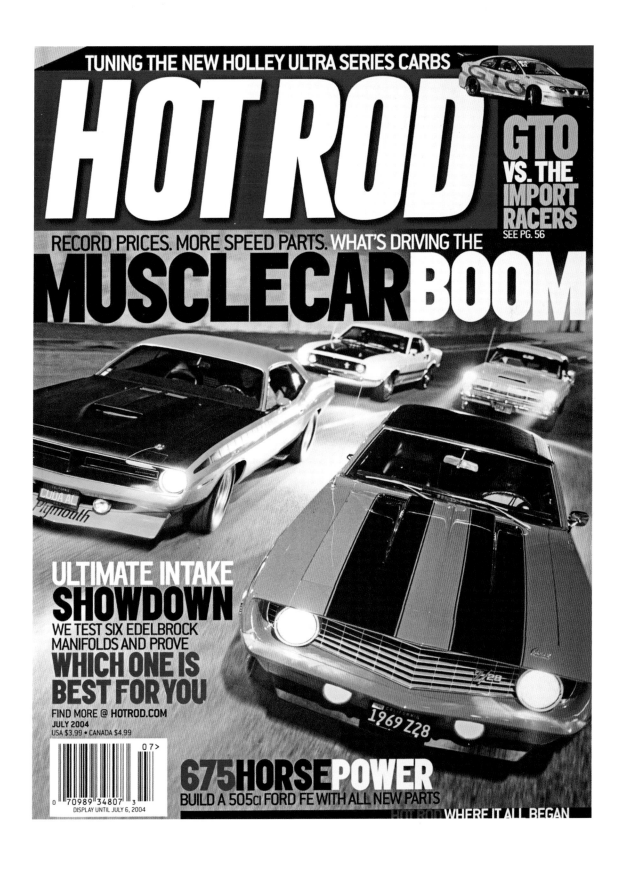

TUNING THE NEW HOLLEY ULTRA SERIES CARBS

HOT ROD

GTO VS. THE IMPORT RACERS
SEE PG. 56

RECORD PRICES. MORE SPEED PARTS. WHAT'S DRIVING THE

MUSCLECAR BOOM

ULTIMATE INTAKE
SHOWDOWN
WE TEST SIX EDELBROCK
MANIFOLDS AND PROVE
WHICH ONE IS
BEST FOR YOU

FIND MORE @ HOTROD.COM

JULY 2004
USA $3.99 • CANADA $4.99

07>

0 70989 34807 3
DISPLAY UNTIL JULY 6, 2004

675 HORSEPOWER
BUILD A 505ci FORD FE WITH ALL NEW PARTS

HOT ROD WHERE IT ALL BEGAN

8490 AND 6420

Petersen always had a knack for real estate, and he never hesitated to jump on the opportunity to buy a worthwhile property at a good price. Sometimes it was a house or a small office building out of which to operate smaller PPC departments, such as advertising sales or circulation. As the company outgrew 5959 Hollywood Boulevard, various segments of the operation scattered in these types of smaller outposts around Los Angeles and Hollywood. In the late 1960s, Petersen seized on the opportunity to acquire a high-rise office building at 8490 Sunset Boulevard in Hollywood. It was large enough to hold the entire PPC operation and included underground parking and a photo studio. First shown on the *Hot Rod* masthead as Petersen Publishing's headquarters in July 1968, it was considered by most longtime employees as the cultural center and most enduring home of Petersen Publishing Company. It was ideally located in the heart of the Sunset Strip, offering a front-row view of the Hollywood Hills and southern views clear to Long Beach and the Pacific Ocean. Not a lavish structure, the building was stately, befitting a premier publishing house.

The building was known for many things, including epic office parties and other escapades. The lobby's "host greeter" always served as a topic of conversation: a large white polar bear, felled by Petersen on an Alaskan hunting trip (using only a .357 Magnum handgun, if you can imagine that), stuffed and standing tall under a spotlight in the Sunset Boulevard lobby.

The location at 8490 Sunset remained PPC's HQ until 1993, when Petersen acquired another high-rise, this one at 6420 Wilshire Boulevard in the mid-Wilshire area of Los Angeles. By the end of 1993, the entire company moved to the new headquarters. This proved an opportune move, as what would become the Petersen Automotive Museum just a few years later was within walking distance on Wilshire Boulevard, a few blocks to the east, at the western edge of L.A.'s Museum Row.

The space could have worked longer as the company's headquarters, but the property was getting old and the land it sat on was worth more than the structure. The once-beloved HQ was bulldozed in 2014 to make way for a new residential and entertainment center called Sunset La Cienega.

At last, the company moved to 6420 Wilshire Boulevard. This was the final property to serve as home for PPC while the Petersens were alive, containing the Petersens' offices, their foundations, and their various holdings.

OPPOSITE: A look up La Cienega Avenue toward the iconic Petersen Publishing building. The *Hot Rod* 25th Anniversary could be seen from all over Los Angeles. Check out some of the cool cars on that day in 1970; you can't miss the big 1967 Lincoln Continental sedan front and center with a Triumph TR6 just behind, then a Fiat 850 Spider followed by an early '60s Plymouth Valient station wagon—and don't miss the Buick Electra 225 partially visible at right. *Petersen Photo Archive/TEN: The Enthusiast Network*

This great photo accomplishes at least two things; it demonstrates that *Hot Rod* and Petersen Photographic staffers will go anywhere to get the shot, and it's also a sky-high temporary billboard to advertise the magazine. This is staffer Eric Rickman, wielding his trusty Hassleblad roll film camera, at 1965 NHRA Winternationals in Pomona, California, as captured by *Rod & Custom*'s Darryl Norenberg. *Petersen Photo Archive/TEN: The Enthusiast Network*

HOT ROD'S 50TH CELEBRATION

OPPOSITE: 6420 Wilshire Boulevard, Los Angeles: The last and final home for what was Petersen Publishing Company and Mr. and Mrs. Petersen's executive offices. This handsome high-rise has since been sold, remodeled, and renamed. *Petersen Photo Archive/TEN: The Enthusiast Network*

ABOVE: Petersen Publishing always celebrated its major milestones in meaningful ways; this is the cover of the invite to *Hot Rod*'s 50th Anniversary celebration party at the SEM show in 1998. The illustration was commissioned to honor the car on the cover of the first January 1948 issue. *Petersen Photo Archive/TEN: The Enthusiast Network*

RIGHT: Robert E. Petersen once commented that he was surprised *Hot Rod* even "made it past the first few issues." Fortunately, he was around to see and enjoy the title's 50th birthday in January 1998. This isn't the actual car that appeared on the first cover, but a specially commissioned replica built for the occasion. It sat in the Petersen Building lobby for several years. *Petersen Photo Archive/TEN: The Enthusiast Network*

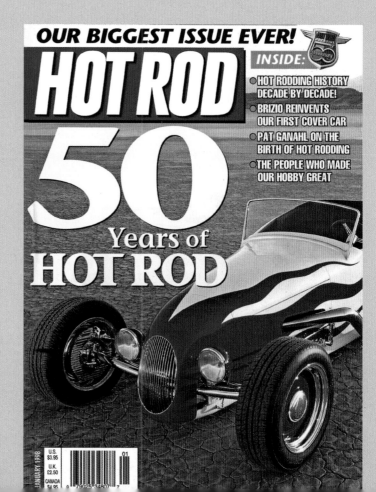

OUR BIGGEST ISSUE EVER!

HOT ROD

50 Years of HOT ROD

INSIDE:
- HOT RODDING HISTORY DECADE BY DECADE!
- BRIZIO REINVENTS OUR FIRST COVER CAR
- PAT GANAHL ON THE BIRTH OF HOT RODDING
- THE PEOPLE WHO MADE OUR HOBBY GREAT

JANUARY 1998

U.S. $3.95
U.K. £2.50
CANADA $4.95

01

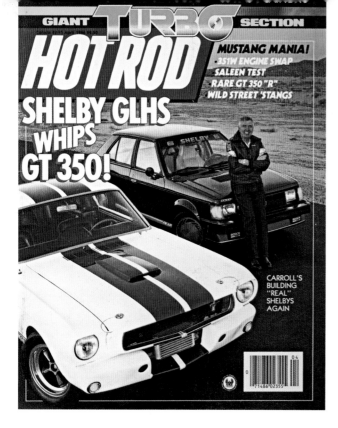

On the cover:

GIANT TURBO SECTION

HOT ROD

MUSTANG MANIA!
- 351W ENGINE SWAP
- SALEEN TEST
- RARE GT 350 "R"
- WILD STREET 'STANGS

SHELBY GLHS WHIPS GT 350!

CARROLL'S BUILDING "REAL" SHELBYS AGAIN

ABOVE: The incomparable Carroll Shelby goes back into the car business with Chrysler this time instead of Ford, and makes the cover of *Hot Rod* with his Omni GLHS and a Shelby GT350 Mustang; the latter is much more "old school" *Hot Rod* magazine fodder, while the front-drive, turbocharged, four-cylinder powered Dodge is something new for the magazine's audience circa mid-1986. *Petersen Photo Archive/TEN: The Enthusiast Network*

OPPOSITE TOP: The famous *Hot Rod* Swimsuit Issue concept lasted longer than anyone thought it would, and although it was ultimately judged to be no longer appropriate, the idea sure sold a lot of magazines at the time. *Petersen Photo Archive/TEN: The Enthusiast Network*

OPPOSITE BOTTOM: Sizzling Swimsuits was the theme for 1989's swimsuit special. The concept likely died for the last time in 2015 when The Enthusiast Network company management banned scantily clad women from the pages of all former Petersen titles. *Petersen Photo Archive/TEN: The Enthusiast Network*

continued from page 104

The magazine also covered pickups, sedans, and even station wagons of this ilk. Apart from the already popular 1955–1957 Chevrolet Nomad two-door sport wagon body style, most considered a run-down two-door or four-door wagon from those years as little more than a parts car, something to be robbed of its reusable bits and body panels for rebuilding a more popular two-door, hardtop, or convertible '55–'57. *Hot Rod* showed that these less popular styles could be just as fast, just as cool, as the hot and popular configurations. And that remains true today. The magazine encouraged readers to think outside the shoebox (a nickname for '55–'57 Chevrolets) and build up an Olds, Buick, or Pontiac, all of which shared similar body and chassis architecture.

Hot Rod also promoted trends in low-buck building, ways to make more horsepower for less money and create more affordable cars; these ultimately helped hot rodders build and finish out a car that still looks and runs great without spending the money on the biggest, best, largest-possible engine. This lower-budget approach also included using spray-can detailing instead of expensive trips to the chrome shop. Low-buck and budget building have remained popular themes in *Hot Rod* ever since.

Highlighting every employee who worked at *Hot Rod* or Petersen Publishing would be impossible, but there were many memorable individuals along the way, and there's little question that every one of us who's done a stint there shares a bond. Over time, you could say it was a family. As Eric Dahlquist once told me:

Working at Petersen wasn't a job; it was more like belonging to a club—not a country club mind you, because we worked hard and often long days, weeks, months, and years—and when we played, we played hard. There were all the usual twists and turns you'd find in any society, little cliques and fiefdoms here and there, and office politics certainly made and ended more than a few careers.

Longtime *Motor Trend* road tester and staff writer Chuck Koch also described what it was like:

It was fun to go to work, because we were always doing interesting things with cars, and going great places: road trips, the races, auto shows, factories, carmaker HQs, and such. Plus you never knew who you were going to end up spending the day with. All sorts of Hollywood, car industry types, and other cool folks, were always in and out of the offices. One year, Dan Gurney was on our Car of the Year Jury and testing panel, so we'd go out and drive cars, and eat burgers, and hang out all day with Dan Gurney or Parnelli Jones.

Everyone who ever worked there certainly has stories to tell. The late Mike Anson, who worked at several Petersen titles over time, once commented that, "if we ever hold a true Petersen

continued on page 118

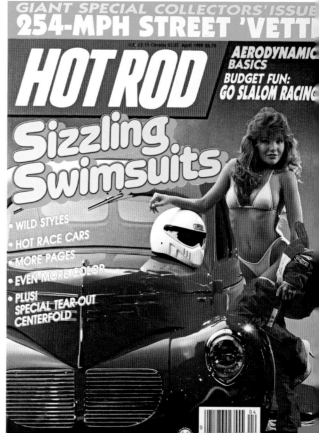

THE MAGNIFICENT DOZEN:
THE 12 (OR SO) MOST INFLUENTIAL HRM STAFFERS

In the January 2018 issue of *Hot Rod*, David Freiburger summarized his top eight most influential staffers. We agree with all of his selections—"but wait, there's more." In a riff on his original list, we've expanded it slightly, for a list that could easily run many more pages. Trying to weight their significance is impossible, so they're given here in alphabetical order.

GRAY BASKERVILLE

"Your Old Dad" Baskerville joined the company in 1967 and moved to *Rod & Custom* five years later, sidestepping to *Hot Rod* when *R&C* morphed into *HRM* in 1974. David Freiburger calls him "the most loved and remembered editorial staff member, holding his ground at the grassroots level," though he never become editor in chief. He drove a very cool '32 Ford hot rod; his usual work attire was shorts, a Hawaiian shirt, and flip-flops; and he also acquitted himself well as a photographer. Gray passed on in 2002.

Gray Baskerville

JOHN DIANNA

This drag racer and hot rodder first worked as a vacuum cleaner salesman at Sears. He joined *Hot Rod* in 1968, climbing the ladder through editor and publisher positions at *Car Craft, Motor Trend*, and *Hot Rod* before becoming a major-league editorial director for dozens of automotive titles. He was a polarizing figure in the history of modern specialty publishing, but many of his decisions and direct hires impacted the company for decades. He passed away in 2016.

Robert E. Petersen (left) and Ray Brock

RAY BROCK

Known as the "tall, bald guy from *Hot Rod*," Brock joined the roster in 1953. A serious and committed hot rodder and racer, he was also a great talker and a natural salesman. He had a long career, serving on both the editorial and sales/advertising/business sides of Petersen Publishing Company. He passed away in 2002.

MARLON DAVIS AND STEVE MAGNANTE

Davis in 2017 notched his fortieth anniversary as a *Hot Rod* staffer, most of them spent as its technical editor. He was already a gearhead at a young age. He knew how to work his race cars—he was a natural—and got in the door thanks to being somebody's neighbor (isn't that always how it happens?). He's been generating, photographing, and writing technical features since joining PPC in 1977.

Magnante is a diehard drag racer who builds altered-wheelbase Funny Cars in his own garage. He also worked at *Hot Rod* as a technical editor from August 1997 to January 2004. Since he left, he's authored several books about cars, and has enjoyed a successful career on a variety of automotive television programs.

Marlon Davis

BOB D'OLIVO

After Mr. Petersen, D'Olivo was *Hot Rod's* first real photographer. He joined in late 1952 and cast the die for what became Petersen Photographic Services. D'Olivo remains a friend of the house, often filling in the blanks about this old photo or that. He brought serious technical photography skills to PPC.

Bob D'Olivo

DAVID FREIBURGER

This highly influential and visionary editor, leader, and content creator absolutely deserves to be on his own list. He's been the editor in chief for more issues of *Hot Rod* than any other editor. He joined the staff in December 1991, serving long and strong as its editorial leader from 2001 to 2013, with a year out in the middle to help launch an internet startup. He remains on the masthead today as a senior vice president and columnist.

PAT GANAHL

The cool-thinking and talented Ganahl is a superb editor and gifted writer. In 2017, staffer Thom Taylor dubbed Ganahl "the editor with the distinction of holding that position for the least amount of time: nine months. 'Too-Tall' Pat Ganahl is the first to admit he knew his days were probably numbered when he took the position. It wasn't from a lack of talent or experience, but maybe a lack of tolerance for office politics." No matter, he's a serious and committed hot rodder, having enjoyed a commendable post-Petersen career as a freelance journalist and hot-rodding book author. He has a big garage full of race cars and hot rod toys he built mostly himself. And his Cadillac-powered '32 Ford highboy roadster is the absolute definition of a traditional hot rod.

LEE KELLY

His college car was a 409-horsepower, 409-cubic-inch '62 Chevrolet Impala SS, so that tells you the kind of fuel that pumps through this guy's heart. Kelly did his time and paid his dues at other hot-rod–related magazines produced by other companies, ending up at Petersen after those early jobs. Kelly is an avid, capable drag racer, running a variety of his own cars over time, and competing at Bonneville and Baja. Kelly was *Motor Trend* group president when I worked there in the late 1990s and early 2000s.

TOM MEDLEY

Medley was the first *Hot Rod* editorial employee other than the "Founding Roberts" (Petersen and Lindsay), joining for the second issue in 1948. As discussed above, he penned the Stoker McGurk comic, among others. For some years, he was the editor and spiritual leader at *Rod & Custom.* Medley was always a happy, fun, and deeply talented guy. He passed away in 2014.

WALLY PARKS

Parks had as much to do with the birth of *Hot Rod* and Petersen Publishing as Petersen and Lindsay. He first got involved through the Southern California Timing Association, which presented the original Hot Rod Exposition in 1948, and was originally billed in the new *Hot Rod* magazine as technical consultant. (Lindsay and Petersen were really the first editors, even though they billed themselves as associate editors.) In 1949, Parks officially joined the magazine as its editor, and he held

Wally Parks

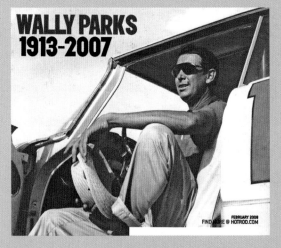

WALLY PARKS
1913-2007

FEBRUARY 2008
FIND MORE @ HOTROD.COM

that position until the early 1960s. He and Petersen put their heads together to found the NHRA, which organized and changed the face of drag racing from a "thug sport" to a professional motorsport. Parks insisted that hot rodding could be safe and fun, which informed many of his activities at the beginning. The NHRA Museum in Pomona, California, is properly named in his honor.

ROBERT E. PETERSEN

As we've seen throughout this book, Petersen was the central figure behind *Hot Rod,* the title he cofounded in 1948. He passed away in 2007.

Robert E. Petersen

ERIC RICKMAN

Like Bob D'Olivo, "Rick" was a superb shooter, particularly good at the high-speed action photography needed at the racetrack. He freelanced for the magazine from the very beginning, joined as a staffer in 1952, and stayed on until 1970, when he began shooting motorcycles for PPC's bike books. An original member of the NHRA Drag Safari team, Rick retired in 1992. He set up his darkroom in the sky in 2008.

A. B. SHUMAN

Besides being a committed hot rodder, racer, and car guy, Arnold Baer Shuman had top-notch skills as a writer. A lifelong hot rodding enthusiast, "A. B." was with *Hot Rod's* sister publications, *Car Craft* and *Motor Trend,* before hopping across the hall to become *Hot Rod's* editor in the early 1970s. He was one of the auto industry's best-known and most-respected PR professionals. Shuman graduated Tufts University in 1962, then spent five years in the Navy as a pilot; he joined Petersen Publishing in 1967. After *Hot Rod,* he joined Mercedes-Benz and was responsible for public relations and press information at the automaker for nearly twenty-five years, until his retirement in 1995. He succumbed to injuries suffered in a slip-and-fall accident in 2013.

Ed Iskenderian (left) and A. B. Shuman

Publishing Company reunion, and if everyone still around could show up, we'd need to rent Dodger Stadium or the L.A. Coliseum to hold it." There is an impromptu "class reunion" that takes place at the Westgate Hotel bar in Las Vegas every year during the SEMA show, and it's a come-one, come-all, no-host gathering of handshakes, drinks, remembrances, and storytelling about the good old—and occasionally bad old—days of PPC.

Former staffer Charles Daniel Ross put it succinctly: "Anyone who worked at PPC at any time in its history will tell you their tenure was the best time of their lives. We all feel the same way, across the many decades."

HOT ROD *IN THE '80S*

Hot Rod—and hot rodding—continued to face challenges throughout the 1970s. Tighter regulations and stricter equipment requirements combined with other major stumbling blocks, such as the alleged gas shortages of 1973 and 1979 that reinforced fuel economy mandates. By the 1980s, though, changes were on the way that every hot rodder could celebrate.

Model year 1982 provides a good example: Ford's reintroduced Mustang GT offered a newly engineered and more powerful 5.0-liter (302-cubic-inch) V-8 with a manual transmission package, signalling the return of performance to the lineup. This was one of the first models in the modern era where an American carmaker paid attention to the underhood appearance of the engine and engine bay. Instead of just spraying the whole area with flat black paint or coating the engine with a gallon of "Ford Blue," the engineers and designers used more naturally finished metals

Petersen's creative and aggressive advertising execs often bundled various groups of like titles together in order to sell large ad buys across a wide variety of reader demographics. It is clear that this mid-90s brochure was targeting a male audience by offering group ad buys for *Hot Rod, Motor Trend, Car Craft, Motorcyclist, Guns & Ammo, Hunting, Skin Diver,* and *Photographic. Petersen Foundation Collection*

hose routing, and other details to make the engine compartment look smarter. General Motors introduced smaller, lighter, faster, and better-handling Chevrolet Camaro and Pontiac Firebird Trans Am models, also with an eye to bringing back from-the-factory performance.

Positive changes got easier as carmakers developed better emission control hardware, fuel injection, and more precise computerized engine management systems that allowed engines to produce more power and run more efficiently than most of the cars of the mid- to late-1970s. And the performance aftermarket, largely through the efforts of SEMA's political action and lobbyists, learned to get along better with government regulators in the interests of improving performance and meeting more stringent emissions and fuel economy requirements. All of this was good news for performance car enthusiasts, hot rodders, and racers alike.

Throughout the 1980s, *Hot Rod* continued to experiment in its search for a voice and place in the new world. Something new for 1987 was the Swimsuit Issue, riffing on the original "Parts with Appeal" theme of the 1950s. This time, though, it was much racier and in full color, with page after page of dazzling young swimsuit models draped in, around, and over hot rods and race cars of all stripes. *Playboy* magazine had certainly proven that sex sells, and *Hot Rod* didn't have as much automotive performance to sell on the newsstand as it used to, so the car title gave this approach a try. These issues sold well enough, but they weren't what the magazine or movement was all about; the concept eventually ran its course and hasn't been repeated since 2015.

Not that attractive women disappeared from the cover of *Hot Rod*. Even though the Swimsuit Spectacular (as it was known in later years)

In addition to repackaging its editorial materials into special edition magazines, the company had a books division that created all manner of special titles. There was so much editorial power on staff that it only made sense to leverage every specialty interest outlet possible. *Petersen Photo Archive/TEN: The Enthusiast Network*

ABOVE LEFT: Petersen Publishing was the master of creating one-shot or special edition magazine and books centered around one subject and/or aimed at a specific audience. Often the material was culled from previously published issues and magazines, yet a surprising amount of the editorial was created from scratch for these special titles. A very smart way to get more mileage out of editorial content and targeted marketing—today we call it repurposing. *Petersen Photo Archive/ TEN: The Enthusiast Network*

ABOVE RIGHT: Here's an example of the variety of special and technical editions produced by Petersen Publishing in the 1970s—you'll recognize a lot of nameplates no longer in production, such as Ford's Pinto, the Chevrolet Vega, Datsun (which of course became Nissan), and Plymouth, also no longer produced. *Petersen Photo Archive/TEN: The Enthusiast Network*

had enjoyed its moment in the sun, there was an occasional "Miss *Hot Rod*" or complimentary "Miss *Hot Rod*" poster or calendar giveaway. (At this point we should make clear that, while many women enjoy cars and hot rodding, it would be misguided to say that the primary *Hot Rod* audience was not assumed to be male.) Freebies modeled on the "Parts with Appeal" theme, polybagged with a regular issue, proved popular on the newsstand and often resulted in strong issue sales.

DAVID FREIBURGER AND BEYOND

As we've seen, *Hot Rod* has enjoyed several legendary leaders as editors in chief, but one of the most visionary and influential in recent years was David Freiburger. He launched his automotive career with a position at a Dodge dealership parts counter immediately after high school, then moved to a machine shop.

He finally landed at Petersen Publishing in 1991 as a *Hot Rod* staff editor, becoming editor in chief in 2001 and remaining in that position until 2013. He freely admits that his predecessors, including Wally Parks and Robert Petersen himself, were huge influences on how he ran, and ultimately reinvented, *Hot Rod* magazine. Freiburger wrote:

It's fair to say that anyone working in the performance industry today can trace their career to the influence of Robert E. Petersen. More importantly, consider all the millions of people he made happy over the past 60 years bringing the best of their hobbies into their homes every month. Even now, a week does not pass when I don't hear a story of how the Hot Rod *of the Petersen era influenced people's lives for the better.*

A senior editorial manager at The Enthusiast Network, the company that currently owns and publishes *Hot Rod* and a large roster of former PPC titles as of this writing, Freiburger added:

[I'm] proud to have worked for Petersen. [Subsequent editor Rob] Kinnan and I will be the last Hot Rod *editors to have been hired under his ownership. Even so, I didn't truly know the man . . . . I'd occasionally run into him in the lobby or elevator . . . We called him Uncle Pete behind his back, and Mr. Petersen to his face—never Bob, Pete or Boss, as he was known by those closer to him. He'd occasionally show up at the quarterly business meetings for magazines I worked on, and was usually a quiet specter unless he felt the need to cut the BS with pointed directives that revealed his acumen.*

This 1969 issue of Petersen's *Hot Rod* Industry News featured a full wrap up on the SEMA industry trade show, which even by then had grown into one of the largest professional trade shows in America; it is today among the largest in the world. *Petersen Foundation Collection*

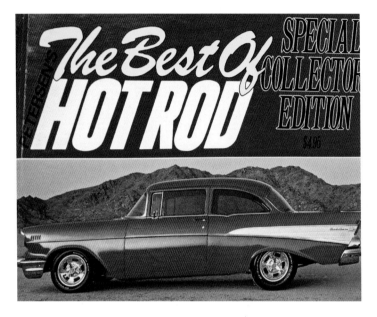

OPPOSITE: This is a great little book for anyone looking to understand or get deeper into hot rodding culture. It's a compendium of articles and work authored by a number of big names in hot rodding, including several former *Hot Rod* magazine staffers, and the Boss himself, Robert E. Petersen. Charming stuff, and a must have for any serious or new fan of hot rodding. *Author collection*

Later, at industry functions and parties, he was more approachable. I had made it to the Hot Rod *Editor's chair by the time I introduced myself to him and Margie at the 25th Anniversary of the Street Machine Nationals, and he responded with, "I know who you are." I should have suspected that.*

I asked him if he had any advice on running the magazine, and he said, "Have fun and keep it clean. If you're having fun, everything else works out." At the time, having been through two ownership changes and massive budget cuts, we were not having fun, and it showed. Badly. When we finally invested in the magazine and revamped it in mid-2004 [centered on the theme of "Where It All Began"], I was especially proud when word came from Petersen's office that he was pleased with what we had done. Our team had lunch with him once at The Palm restaurant, and we pummeled him with questions about stories we'd heard from the heyday.

As this book goes to print, *Hot Rod* is preparing to publish its seventieth anniversary issue. Under solid and committed management, the magazine appears set for many more decades of leadership in the hot rodding editorial space. *Hot Rod* has understandably made a big deal of milestones and published special issues around its anniversaries; at times there have been huge industry and employee parties to mark the occasions.

Besides all the cars, car museums, and car magazines, the Petersens were fascinating people on many levels, and while much of what they did centered on automobiles and their publishing business, there was much more to them than that.

THE Hot Rod Reader

Stories of Hot Rodding and
Kustom Kulture from Gray Baskerville,
Ed Roth, Wally Parks, Dean Batchelor,
Robert E. Petersen, and many more!

Edited by Melinda Keefe and Peter Schletty

EVERYTHING'S A PROJECT

Project cars are common in the car magazine business. Special cars built with, by, or for a given title, they're often race cars that help heavy-footed staffers scratch their itch for speed. They foster all kinds of editorial content and great (though sometimes disastrous) storytelling along the way. Some project builds come out of junkyards or staffers' garages, others from race shops, and some begin life as brand-new cars provided to the magazine by carmakers as a marketing exercise. Over the decades, *Hot Rod* has built, wrecked, raced, restored, and otherwise participated in a bunch of these projects. Here are a few worth remembering.

CABALLO I AND II

Many of *Hot Rod*'s most memorable race car projects involved Alexander Kennedy "A. K." Miller. He was a hot rodder, car and engine builder, shop owner, and racing driver of note. The idea for his Caballo de Hierro ("Iron Horse") race cars was to build them hot-rodder style. Junkyard dogs built out of a bunch of leftover parts that seemingly shouldn't fit together, these cars were relatively light and always fast. Caballo I was based on a narrowed and reworked 1950 Ford frame, over which sat a fendered and modified Model T "Turtle Deck" body. It also included a bunch of other random parts, including a suitably amped-up 357-cubic-inch Oldsmobile V-8 running four carburetors. Not content to attempt a little drag racing or even a run at Bonneville, A. K. and a bunch of the guys from Petersen Publishing took the tooth-grilled, *Hot Rod*–sponsored race rod

OPPOSITE: Il Caballo I and crew in a charmingly posed team shot in Mexico, prior to the start of the Carrera Panamericana in 1954. We don't know the names of all the guys in this shot, but that's Robert E. Petersen at far left, Ray Brock in the middle, A. K. Miller at the wheel, and "co-piloto" Doug Harrison in the shotgun seat. *Petersen Photo Archive/TEN: The Enthusiast Network*

This garage shot gives you a closeup perspective of Caballo I's homebuilt rig: the wheels are steel (not the fancy knockoff wires run by the Ferraris), the windshield is a frameless piece of glass from who knows what, and the homemade grille mesh is held in place with zip ties. Hot Rod's Ray Brock is second from left, co-driver Doug Harrison is third from left, A. K. Miller in darker overalls and crew cut is fourth from left, and a slim, trim Robert E. Petersen stands tall at far right. *Petersen Photo Archive/TEN: The Enthusiast Network*

to Mexico to contest the Carrera Panamericana on- and off-road race in 1954. They were running against a roster full of purpose-built racing cars and high-dollar European sports cars specially modified for the grueling Mexican enduro. In spite of a raft of problems that necessitated near nightly rebuilds and repairs, A. K.'s Number 11 finished in a more-than-commendable fifth place, behind a quartet of Ferraris.

I begat II. Building on the lessons learned (and with a few of the parts from Caballo I), Miller and his merry band of fabricators got a little more serious with a new car for 1957. This one was based on a purpose-built tubular chassis, with a shapely aluminum body that resembled OSCAs and Maseratis of the period. Caballo II got a larger, hotter engine, too, in the form of a high-compression 392-cubic-inch Chrysler Hemi V-8 running a Hilborn fuel injection system. With high-speed gearing in the rear diff, Caballo II could hit an astonishing 180 miles per hour—really sailing for a home-built racer in the late 1950s. Political issues prevented the running of the Carrera Panamerica that year, so A. K. and the boys decided to take a bite of an even more prestigious open road endurance race, Italy's Mille Miglia event, which

Wally Parks gives a hearty wave out the window of the "Suddenly" Plymouth. The aerodynamic headlight covers have an obvious homemade look about them—one wonders how truly aero-efficient they were—though the Moon disc wheels likely helped reduce drag. *Petersen Photo Archive/TEN: The Enthusiast Network*

Jerry Unser's *Hot Rod* Ford won its class in 1957 but didn't fare so well the following year, as evidenced by the modified bodywork in this post-'58 race photo. Luckily nobody was hurt, but no records set that year, either. *Petersen Photo Archive/TEN: The Enthusiast Network*

ran from Brescia to Rome and back through fast and dangerous mountain passes. A brake drum failed big-time at about the 300-mile mark, taking Caballo II out of the race. In spite of its DNF at the Mille, Caballo II went on to straight-line competition at Bonneville, and it also tore up the SCCA road courses at Palm Springs and the then-new Riverside International Raceway.

THE SUDDENLY 1957 PLYMOUTH SAVOY

Plymouth's ad campaign for its big, finned 1957 models was "Suddenly, it's 1960," promoting what the company felt was its edgy and advanced design language. This is how the car earned its nickname, "Suddenly." It was probably as aerodynamic as a side-by-side refrigerator/freezer, but it packed big power in the form of a suitably amped-up Chrysler Hemi, said to be good for more than 500 horsepower if enough nitromethane was added to the fuel mix. Wally Parks raced it on the beach at Daytona, setting an impressive sedan-class two-way-average record at just a fuzz over 160 miles per hour. Ray Brock ran the car at Bonneville, with an even hotter engine running a now-lethal mix of nitro in the gas, and the engine grenaded while running over 180 miles per hour, negating the record attempt and the car's forays on the salt. Even though the *Hot Rod*–sponsored car was a '57, it ran race number x1960, further tying it to the factory's ad campaign. A great big car that made great big power—until it went great big kaboom.

With the exception of the mildly increased ride height, Cragar SS wheels, and skid plate visible just below the front bumper, it would be hard to tell the *Hot Rod* Ranchero from dead stock—but that was the premise of Baja's stock classes back then. Good prep and smooth but fast-enough driving allowed for class wins two years running. *Petersen Photo Archive/TEN: The Enthusiast Network*

The Turck/Freiburger Camaro has often blistered the salt, in this photo sponsored by *Hot Rod* and TEN title Road Kill. It has since run even faster than the *Hot Rod* editor's record run, which put him solidly in Bonneville's 200 MPH Club. *Petersen Photo Archive/TEN: The Enthusiast Network*

1957 FORD FAIRLANE PIKES PEAK RACER

Further demonstrating that *Hot Rod* was into more than just straight-line racing, Petersen and the magazine sponsored Jerry Unser's Ford sedan racer for the Pikes Peak Hill Climb events in 1957. It was packing a supercharged Ford 312 Y-block V-8 with a factory-stock, 300-horsepower rating, but who knows how many ponies this Louis Unser–built engine actually cranked out. It was good enough to get the eldest of the original Unser brothers up "America's Mountain" in a stock sedan class record of 15:23.7.

1968 FORD RANCHERO

Off-road racing on the Baja California Peninsula was born in the mid-1960s and grew in form and popularity to the point of becoming two events, the Baja 500 and Baja 1000. In the beginning, the hot times were set on motorcycles, then on race-built dune buggies, until Parnelli Jones and Bill Stroppe rewrote the record books with a crazy-fast, tube-framed Ford Bronco known as "Big Oly." As more types of vehicles began to show up to run Baja, the organizers established classes to make room for and welcome all the varieties of hardware. Ray Brock teamed up—again—with A. K. Miller to run a well-prepped and mildly modified Ranchero in the two-wheel-drive "production" class in the 1967 thousand-mile event. Equipped with a 390 V-8 with automatic trans, the car/truck won its class in record time that year, then backed it up with another class-winning run in 1968 that took 6.8 hours off the winning time from the year before.

THE TURK AND FREIBURGER 1980 CAMARO

Editor David Freiburger wanted to join Bonneville's prestigious 200 MPH Club, which involves much more than filling out an application and paying dues. Earning your membership card takes nothing less than safely and successfully making at least two passes at over 200 miles per hour. David teamed up with Keith and Tonya Turk, who brought their race-built 1980 Camaro to the salt. Freiburger's stake was to build his own engine in the form of a blown, small-block Chevy V-8 that, even after some trials and tribulations during testing, helped Freiburger and the Camaro "join the club," running a 243.015-mile-per-hour average for the two runs. That's 200-plus and into the club, with over 40 miles per hour to spare, and the car has since run over 260. It was an all-time *Hot Rod* project car favorite, for sure.

TRUCKS AND VANS

A company that's always travelling to and from events, or putting them on, and covering shows and races will naturally need support vehicles. For PPC, many of them became rolling billboards for the company—or at least for the company's magazine titles. This Chevrolet panel van appeared to be factory stock and not hot-rodded or modified in any way other than being one of those billboards advertising PPC and many of its titles. Many such rigs came and went over the decades.

5

Planes, (No Trains), Automobiles, and Other Personal Pursuits

E ven though cars and their businesses were the center of their world, Margie and Pete were deeply involved in many different ventures, as described in the following interview by longtime Petersen staffer Fred M. H. Gregory:

Together, the Petersens spend most evenings and weekends at charity or business affairs. "We're in so many different things," Bob says.

"On weekends, we'll be with a bunch of skin-diving guys; another weekend we'll be at a race in Daytona and another time we'll be with a group of boat guys. A lot of our fun and our friends have come out of the business," says Margie. "We're exposed to the most interesting people in the whole world," but whenever they can, they go off by themselves for some quiet time at the ranch [they also owned a sprawling, Western-style ranch in the desert hills just south of Palmdale, California] or on the boat.

"We never run out of things to talk about," Margie says.

"Some of the talk is about the future. We're looking for some nice things to do," Bob says. "We're pretty deep into a lot of charities."

OPPOSITE: Mr. and Mrs. Petersen on the driveway of their elegant Beverly Hills home with some of their cars, bikes, and other motorized toys. We're not sure of their connection to the Gary Gabelich racing car at left, but you'll note Mr. P.'s prized Lamborghini Espada, a dune buggy, several motorcycles, and a customized camper van conversion (never forgetting what outdoorsy types the Petersens were), with Mrs. Petersen's Mercedes-Benz 450SL roadster in the background. Judging from the model years of some of the cars, and Mr. and Mrs. P.'s clothing and hairstyles, we estimate this photo was taken in 1973 or 1974. *Petersen Photo Archive/TEN: The Enthusiast Network*

A great deal of their time and money goes to the Thalians, Boys Clubs, the Los Angeles Music Center, and other worthy causes, but not to the neglect of the business that makes all the good works possible.

Bob's hobbies came to be reflected by his magazines: skin diving, boating, hunting, and photography among them. "I could have put out a magazine like Playboy," he reflects. "But I feel I should do what fits me, and what I like, and what suits my personality."

The Petersens' motor yacht was named Sea Rod, an oceangoing ode to *Hot Rod* magazine. An avid sportsman, boating enthusiast, and big game fisherman, Mr. Petersen loved to take the twin-engine boat out with the family or entertain friends and business associates. *Petersen Foundation collection*

As you can imagine, the Petersens were spectacular entertainers and hosts. Their magnificent, yet somehow warmly cozy Beverly Hills home at 625 Mountain Drive was the site of many parties—some purely social, some for charity fundraising—and much of the credit for the success of all these gatherings goes to "house manager" Nancy Reddin, who worked hard to make sure "all the trains ran on time." We think of her as house manager because "housekeeper" doesn't begin to cover the scope of things she did as part of the Petersen household. (Although not related to them, this lovely Irish lady was very much family.)

The Petersens had the touch for hosting and entertaining. Gigi Carleton remembers how responsibility for executing on details often fell to her:

It didn't matter if it was a party for friends at their house, or the Petersen Publishing Company Party at the SEMA show, or at a major auto show— the Petersens always wanted every detail just right, and the comfort and enjoyment of their guests came first.

ABOVE, LEFT, AND FOLLOWING PAGES:
Mr. Petersen and his Vignale-bodied Maserati Spyder appeared in a television commercial and print ad campaign for Ballantine's Scotch whiskey company; the shoot took place at Riverside Raceway. It's clearly one of his favorite cars, used to market what was reputedly one of his favorite drinks. *Petersen Photo Archive/TEN: The Enthusiast Network*

Journalist/author/historian Ken Gross, who later served as executive director of the Petersen Automotive Museum, commented:

Margie always had a great sense of occasion; she knew just when and how to set up a photo op among any group of people; she'd figure out who should be standing next to who, and of course, she always looked perfect for the camera—all of this showed her modeling experience at play. And if you ever needed to know who the best caterer in L.A. was for a given event or party, all you ever had to do was ask Margie.

Mr. Petersen often visited carmaker factories and headquarters for a variety of reasons. We don't know if this was the Mercedes-Benz 300SL roadster that ended up in his collection; it may have been one he was just driving for the visit. No matter: Mr. P. clearly knew fine cars, and he owned many of them. *Petersen Photo Archive/TEN: The Enthusiast Network*

CARS, CARS, CARS

Over time, particularly as their wealth increased, the Petersens became deeply involved car collectors. And they didn't just buy flavor-of-the-month cars, or whatever was the most expensive; they chose special cars that meant something to them, and they made the effort to know and learn about what they were buying.

ABOVE AND LEFT: The Petersens also owned one of the hand-built 600 limos, dubbed the "car of kings, and a king among cars." They bought the car new in 1965 and owned it for the rest of their lives. It ultimately wore the California personalized license plate "Scandia," occasionally shuttling very special customers to and from the Scandia restaurant during the Petersens' tenure as its owners. These photos were taken at the *Motor Trend* 500 parade in downtown Riverside, California in 1966. *Petersen Photo Archive/TEN: The Enthusiast Network*

Mr. and Mrs. Petersen owned several Ferraris over the years, including F40 and F50 supercars. They visited the Ferrari factory many times; this photo was taken in 2003 in front of the company's front gate in Maranello, Italy. *Petersen Foundation collection*

I once asked Mr. Petersen about some of his favorite cars. There were many. He spoke of his Vignale-bodied Maserati 3500 GT Spyder, saying that it "was very beautiful, and a lot of fun to drive, although not as well built as the Ferraris of the day or my Mercedes-Benz 300SL roadster." Another favorite was his Lamborghini Espada, which he said was a "good car to take hunting because it was a lot faster and more fun than an old pickup truck, and there was plenty of room in the large hatchback cargo area for guns and gear" . . . along with anything he happened to capture that day. Imagine stuffing a dead deer or a dozen grouse in the back of your Lambo! Mr. P. also commented that he liked the large rear window so he could keep an eye out for "his friends of the California Highway Patrol."

He often bought cars at collector car auctions for himself and for his museums. It was great fun watching him bid, which I did on several occasions. When a lot that he wanted rolled up to the block, he'd sit calmly in the front row, raise his bidder's paddle, and hold it in the air until the gavel fell in his favor. No hooting, no jumping up and down, and no emotional high-fiving—none of the over-the-top behavior we see in today's televised auctions. He'd sit with his paddle held about shoulder high until he won the bid, and would offer a quiet smile when the action was over.

Mr. P. bought and drove several Ferraris; he was absolutely on the factory's list of preferred buyers. He once spoke of visiting the Ferrari factory in the early 1960s and going out for a test drive with Enzo Ferrari himself. Later in life, his daily drivers were commonly larger Ferrari GTs mixed in with the occasional Caddy or Bentley Continental GT coupe. Given his longtime relationship with Carroll Shelby, it's no surprise that he owned many Shelbys over time, mostly Mustang GT350s (although there's no record of him ever owning a Cobra). Mrs. Petersen preferred Mercedes-Benz SL roadsters, and over time she had several.

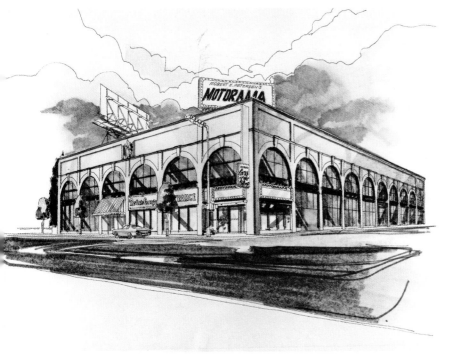

ABOVE: The Petersens felt that any car museum located in or near Los Angeles should focus on and feature movie, TV, and celebrity cars, and that's what Motorama was all about. The exhibits and displays rotated often among cars the Petersens owned, cars from the studios, and cars owned by their celebrity friends. It was a small but mighty place, usually exhibiting 60 to 70 cars at any given time. Lots of fun, inexpensive to visit, and right in the heart of Hollywood. *Petersen Foundation collection*

LEFT: An early rendering of the Motorama building. With its prime corner location, high-ceilinged rooms, and arching window designs, just imagine how it looked in the 1930s as an elegant showroom filled with new Cadillacs and La Salles. It's a shame the Petersens weren't successful in expanding the property and creating a larger, more permanent auto museum in this location. The building now houses a Marshall's department store; it retains much of the building's original period style. *Petersen Foundation collection*

MOTORAMA INFORMATION

LOCATION: 7001 Hollywood Boulevard, Ca 90028, Hollywood, Ca. Adjacent to the Chinese Theater. Across the street from the Hollywood Roosevelt Hotel. Special parking indoors at the hotel. Other parking in two close by lots.

HOURS: Open weekdays 10 a.m. to 10 p.m. Saturday and Sunday, 11 a.m. to 10 p.m.

ADMISSION: $2.50 for adults over 18.
$1.50 for Juniors, 12 through 17.
$ .75 for children 6 to 12.
Free admission children under 6.

Special group prices for school field trips, tourist groups, business and professional adults, church and other fund raising events, including charities. For additional detail call Managing Director's office: (213) 461-2855.

ACCEPTABLE CREDIT CARDS:

American Express   Diners
Bank Americard   Mastercharge

Produced by Motorama, Inc.
A Division of Petersen Publishing Company

HOLLYWOOD MOTORAMA MUSEUM
7001 Hollywood Blvd., Los Angeles, CA 90028
Phone: (213) 461-2855

HOLLYWOOD MOTORAMA MUSEUM

"Where the Cars are the Stars"

MOTORAMA!

WHAT THE WELL DRESSED DRAG RACER WEARS

A Nomex Pierre Cardin jacket of course. Here, Margie Petersen (wife of PPC Chairman R. E. Petersen) helps drag racer Tony Nancy with his, er, "business suit." After Nancy's smoky arrival in the "Revell Liner" we wonder how much he tipped the parking attendant.

Hollywood Premires aren't new, but a premiere which includes a mid-Hollywood Boulevard burnout by Tony Nancy's 1800 horsepower fueler, the "Revell Liner," well that's not exactly commonplace, even in Hollywood. The gala fete was for the grand opening of Robert E. Petersen's Motorama, a permanent display of some of the world's more unusual cars. Mr. Petersen (Chairman of the Board of Petersen Publishing Company) got together with the reknown automobile customizer, George Barris, and soon thereafter, Motorama was born.

The collection is comprised of 60 cars, and the exhibits are changed periodically. The cars on display range from Barris' Batmobile to Caroll Shelby's Number one Cobra, and just about everything else imaginable, as well as some things that are almost unimaginable --such as a Pontiac-powered stagecoach!

Motorama, located one block west of the Chinese Theater on Hollywood Boulevard, Hollywood, California, is open seven days a week.

ABOVE: Motorama's grand opening was held in Hollywood-premiere style. The star-studded affair featured drag racer Tony Nancy laying hundreds of yards of tire-smoking burnout down Hollywood Boulevard to the delight of the crowd—assuredly the longest legal, police-supervised burnout on Hollywood Boulevard ever. The management and guests of the nearby Roosevelt Hotel weren't as delighted, we assume, after the supercharged, fuel-burning Chrysler Hemi in Nancy's rail dragster erupted in thunder, blowing out or cracking dozens of the old structure's windows. For his troubles, Margie Petersen presented Nancy with a Pierre Cardin jacket made of fireproof Nomex. *Petersen Foundation collection*

TOP AND BOTTOM LEFT: Even though everyone called it Motorama, it was officially billed as the Hollywood Motorama Museum. It seems odd now to see a flyer or information brochure for anything that doesn't have a "www.somethingsomethingsomething.com" address at the bottom. *Petersen Foundation collection*

MOTORAMA

In 1975, the Petersens opened the Hollywood Motorama Museum at 7001 Hollywood Boulevard. The building was an elegant property with tall, arching windows—a former Cadillac LaSalle dealership right on the famous Hollywood Walk of Fame. The museum's motto was "Where the Cars are the Stars," which was true. According to author/historian Ken Gross:

You'll remember the name Motorama from the series of annual hot rod and custom car shows that he produced in the early 1950s. These shows packed such noted halls as the Shrine Auditorium and the Pan-Pacific. [Mr.] Petersen recalls, "The trouble was that they were over too soon to attract our city's visitors; five days and we had to fold the tent for another year." The Motorama Museum was open year-round and featured all the elements that packed the annual shows— racing cars, the strange and wonderful custom cars that starred in movies and television, as well as Detroit dream cars, prototypes, and classic and antique cars from America's automotive past. The Motorama Museum did quite well for

Another fascinating Motorama guest was "Black Beauty," the 1966 Chrysler Imperial built and customized for use in *The Green Hornet* TV series by legendary pinstriper and Hollywood car builder Dean Jeffries. *Petersen Foundation collection*

LEFT: A look inside Motorama in 1975 shows two of its more interesting exhibits. In the foreground is the Mercedes-Benz Cabriolet owned by Hitler mistress Eva Braun, billed here as the "most valuable car in the world." Just behind it, in the upper left side of this photo, is the bullet-ridden 1934 Ford V-8 sedan in which Bonnie and Clyde died. *Petersen Foundation collection*

BELOW: One episode of the *Beverly Hillbillies* television series had the family car turned into a drag racer. George Barris built the show's original, and this racy version, seen here at Motorama with Mr. and Mrs. Petersen. *Petersen Foundation collection*

many years, although when Petersen wanted to expand the museum, local politicians prevented it and eventually Motorama closed [in the mid-1980s].

It was an interesting and attractive place, though its museum craft was fairly straightforward with no over-the-top lighting, stanchions, or turntables. Some of the period press releases for Motorama seem a bit humble now, boasting of "Two million dollars' worth of cars on display." Many of the Petersens' own cars, and those they later purchased for their other, more formidable museum project, are each worth that much today.

The building has had several other uses since the museum closed. Altered for retail use, though retaining much of its original window line and look, it now houses a huge Hollywood souvenir shop and a Marshalls clothing store.

ABOVE: Before his days as an Oscar-winning director, a young Ron Howard visits Motorama and tapes an on-camera interview for local television news. *Petersen Foundation collection*

LEFT: Models Tara Verlander, left, and Carol Boyle, right, add even more Hollywood sparkle to Bob Hope's George Barris–built golf cart. The sign on the marquee behind the car reads "Geo[rge] Barris Batmobile & Batcycle TV & Movie Cars: Wild Customs and Over 55 Exciting Cars." Both Barris and Hope were personal friends of the Petersens, so having this car in their museum was a natural match. *Petersen Foundation collection*

SCANDIA

The Petersens were so fond of fine dining that they eventually came to own one of their favorite establishments, a restaurant called Scandia. *Los Angeles* magazine writer Alison Martino described the city's legendary Scandia restaurant this way:

Scandia, an extravagant global cuisine spot at the corner of Sunset Boulevard and Doheny Avenue . . . wasn't just high-end—it was happening. In its heyday, customers would beg, borrow, and steal for a reservation before 11 p.m. It's where Frank Sinatra kept an office upstairs complete with a personal shower; actor Jack Webb held his wedding reception in the main dining room in 1958; and James Garner ate brunch on Sundays while filming The Rockford Files. *The restaurant was even name-dropped in* American Gigolo, *and visited by five American presidents.*

Scandia was an experience from the moment you pulled up to its huge driveway. . . . Opened in 1957, it was originally owned by Ken Hansen. Along with his wife, Tova, he turned the restaurant into a culinary landmark with elegant decor, impeccable service, and delectable Scandinavian and French cuisine . . . .

The Scandia restaurant building was an elegant mid-century modern structure that looked particularly inviting at night. It wasn't unusual to see Frank Sinatra, Cary Grant, or James Garner drive into the porte-cochère, park, and drop in for dinner or a few drinks. *Petersen Foundation collection*

September 8-15, 1988

This Week **Key**

LOS ANGELES & SOUTHERN CALIFORNIA
The leading WEEKLY MAGAZINE of Southland entertainment & dining. Published EVERY Thursday.

Scandia Restaurant owners Robert E. and Margie Petersen in the main dining room of their internationally known restaurant at 9040 Sunset Blvd. in West Hollywood. Scandia has received the Travel/Holiday Award for 36 consecutive years, and the Wine Spectator Award for one of the 13 finest wine cellars in America. Gourmet Scandinavian cuisine is served for lunch, dinner and Sunday brunch. Closed Mondays. Petersen, also a publisher and art gallery owner, and his wife purchased Scandia in 1978 and are both committed to maintaining Scandia's reputation for fine Scandinavian cuisine and service

This Week in Los Angeles and Southern California

Key

April 18 — 25, 1985
For 49 years the leading weekly magazine of Southland entertainment & dining. Every Thursday since 1936.

Margie and Bob Petersen, owners of Scandia Restaurant, for over 36 years a Sunset Boulevard dining landmark, rated as one of the outstanding restaurants of the world by Travel/Holiday Award and ranked by Wine Spectator as having one of the 13 best wine cellars in America.

ABOVE: The pocket-sized "Key" books were locally published city guides for visitors and locals alike who wanted to know was happening around town. Mr. and Mrs. Petersen and their Scandia restaurant were often featured on the cover and inside these popular guidebooks. It's fair to say they were the "Clark Gable and Carole Lombard" of magazine publishers and L.A. business owners. *Petersen Foundation collection*

RIGHT: One of the private dining rooms in the wine cellar at Scandia. Everyone who was anyone visited, held private dinner parties, and closed business and movie deals in these quietly elegant, European-chic spaces. *Petersen Foundation collection*

Mr. and Mrs. Robert E. Petersen,
owners of the world famous Scandia Restaurant,
salute the achievements of Las Floristas.

For that extra special occasion, Scandia's world famous Wine Cellar, as seen in the December 1983 issue of LOS ANGELES Magazine, offers a memorable dining experience for 12 to 16 guests. The beautiful tapestry chairs and magnificent 150 year old European carved sideboard add a touch of Old World elegance to this unique room, which provides the perfect setting for your intimate luncheons and dinner parties.

9040 Sunset Bl. (at Doheny Dr.)
West Hollywood
For Reservations: 278-3555 or 272-9521

In the '80s, Scandia also had an award-winning wine cellar with more than 30,000 bottles. From 1950 to 1980, the restaurant received a number of awards and this write-up in the Los Angeles Times: *'No one is very sure of the definition of a great restaurant, but everyone is sure that Scandia is one . . . It has appeared on every award list that was ever made of Los Angeles restaurants . . . '*

High up on Sunset Strip, the space seemed to float over the twinkling lights of Los Angeles. It was full of paneled wood, copper and brass fixtures, red leather seating, royal blue and white china, and crystal vases. The principal decorations were coats of arms . . . . The restaurant served its last meal on May 4, 1989. Other restaurateurs launched other concepts in the space, but none stayed open long.

The story of how and why the Petersens loved Scandia and ended up owning it is typical of Mr. Petersen's approach to business and life. It certainly helped that he ate there nearly every day, and was justifiably proud of his Danish heritage, as were Scandia's owners, Mr. and Mrs. Hansen.

Back in the day, Petersen ate lunch every Tuesday through Friday at Scandia. It was often joked among PPC employees that Scandia was the de facto Petersen Cafeteria. The restaurant was closed Mondays, so all the regulars went to the Cock 'n Bull a few blocks down the street for their Monday lunch.

After many decades as owner and even head chef, Mr. Hansen told Petersen he was going to sell the restaurant. Mr. P. couldn't imagine Scandia and its tradition of world-class service and food belonging to anyone else, so he told Hansen he would buy it—on the condition that Hansen would stay on and manage the restaurant. But Hansen was an elderly man by this time and he wanted to travel to his beloved Denmark often,

BELOW: Just as Mr. Petersen was ready to pick up a camera to shoot a cover for *Hot Rod* or rev up a car or motorcycle for a run at Bonneville, the Boss was equally game to pick up a burger flipper and run the flat top at Scandia for one of the many charity events hosted by the Petersens there. *Petersen Photo Archive/TEN: The Enthusiast Network*

OPPOSITE: Scandia's founders and original owners couldn't have dreamed of better custodians of the restaurant than Margie and Robert E. Petersen. Elegant, beautiful people who were popular with locals and knew how to run successful businesses, the Petersens enjoyed owning Scandia. While they didn't realize how much work running a landmark service business would be, they were up to the task, never hesitating to host an event there or walk the floor to greet the clientele. *Petersen Foundation collection*

Petersen Aviation was about airplanes, but if the Petersens' name was on something, cars would be involved somewhere. How does this Bentley earn the right to wear the *Hot Rod* license plate? Simple: this Mulsanne Turbo put out hot-rod-level horsepower and torque. The hacienda-style terminal and office structure behind are the buildings that the Petersens constructed for this purpose at the Van Nuys Airport; the complex is still in use today. *Petersen Foundation collection*

so Petersen told him, "No problem. You can come and go as you want, take vacations, just run the restaurant as always and I will pay the bills and you won't have anything to worry about."

Hansen took Petersen up on his offer. Petersen felt his wife Margie might have fun running the restaurant, though, once they saw how much work it required, they retained the existing staff. Sadly, Mr. Hansen suffered a heart attack at the restaurant a couple of years later; he never got to enjoy the retirement travels he'd longed for.

Scandia was the site of the *Motor Trend* Car of the Year awards presentations, PPC Employee Retirement Parties, Chaîne des Rôtisseurs dinners and Chevalier du Tastevin events (both wine societies), and also many of the Petersens' private parties on Monday nights when the restaurant was closed to the public. They also hosted charity dinners at the restaurant. The Petersens ran Scandia for about ten years before they sold it. The building was leveled in 2015 to make way for a new mid-rise Marriott hotel.

PETERSEN AVIATION

A life of constant air travel—to trade shows and locations for hunting and other outdoor activities—gave Mr. Petersen the idea to buy a private jet. He purchased a used Gulfstream II (G-II) in 1989 and, as always, invested in the latest avionics.

He had a full-time pilot, copilot, and aircraft mechanic in a rented hangar at Van Nuys, California. Fortunately, the copilot was also a terrific airplane mechanic, so when the jet was at other airports, he could—and did—fix anything, even in Africa.

Naturally, one Gulfstream jet begat another. Petersen soon learned that the company could get its own serial designations for its aircraft from the FAA, and this new plane wore bespoke tail number N8490RP—8490 for the publishing company's address on Sunset Boulevard, and RP for Robert Petersen. At the same time, pilot Joe McGuire convinced Petersen that he should become a fixed-base operator (FBO) and establish a charter company. (An FBO is granted the rights to operate at an airport and provide fueling, hangar storage, tie-down and parking, aircraft rental, aircraft maintenance, flight instruction, and similar services.) Petersen agreed and found a long-lease property at the Van Nuys Airport. He purchased its lease, demolished the old hangars, and set about creating Petersen Aviation. The terminal and offices included an elegant, handsomely appointed Spanish-style structure. Once his vision was realized, Petersen Aviation had five huge hangars with white floors so clean you could eat off them.

Petersen sold his original G-II and he bought a G-III that had belonged to Frank Sinatra. He purchased a G-IV from the Coca-Cola Company, and a G-IVSP became the final Gulfstream in the fleet. At its peak, the business owned five Gulfstreams, two Hawker 1000s, a Hawker 800, and a Bonanza prop airplane that the crew used primarily as a puddle jumper to run errands. Petersen Aviation was a 24/7, 365-day-a-year business, with sixty employees in 2005.

When there were big trade shows in Dallas, New York, Orlando, or other cities, Petersen took two jet aircraft filled with PPC advertising sales staffers, publishers, and other prominent personalities. Everyone who flew on the Petersen planes

This great aerial shot shows some of the vintage World War II–era warbirds that the Petersens invited to glitter up the aviation company's grand opening with some legit aircraft history. None were towed in, as each was a fully running and functional aircraft; some were owned and flown by pilots who had flown them when they were new. *Petersen Foundation collection*

Mr. P. easily playing the role of big-game CEO aboard one of his Petersen Aviation jets, reviewing his company's products or the next big deal. This is the type of clientele the company courted, which over time flew rock stars, movie stars, and presidential candidates. *Petersen Foundation collection*

became a little spoiled: they never had to go through security lines, and employees' cars, parked in a hangar, were returned to them washed and ready to go. The aviation business connection was a memorable perk for Petersen employees.

Petersen Aviation was sold in 2006, then resold to Signature Aviation. As this book went to press, the aviation business was still at the same facility built by the Petersens at the Van Nuys Airport.

THE INTERNATIONAL CHILI SOCIETY

Carroll Shelby founded the International Chili Society (ICS) at his Terlingua Ranch in southeast Texas in 1967 along with a friend, C. V. Wood. The original intention was to get Shelby's Texas friends together for a light-hearted competition to claim bragging rights: "my chili is better than yours."

Shelby also had a home in Bel Air, California, not far from the Petersens' home. After initiating the idea of a chili cook-off among friends, he asked Petersen to be one of the judges.

One thing led to another, and the ICS was born as a nonprofit organization. Petersen served on the board of directors for many years, and both he and his wife were judges at the ICS Final Chili Cook-Offs held in Southern California and, finally, in Reno, Nevada. Subsequent cook-offs have been held in other states, and the ICS is still a nationwide organization of "chiliheads." You could legitimately say the Petersens were foodies, no matter if it was surf and turf at Scandia or a great bowl of red.

BOBBY AND RICHIE

Up until this point, you've read no mention of the Petersens' heirs, but they had two sons. "Bobby" (Robert Einar Petersen Jr.) was born in February 1964 (a year after the couple married), and "Richie" (Richard Einar Petersen) was born in September of the following year. Recall

Certainly one of the saddest holiday cards ever, showing the Petersen family before it was shattered by the untimely deaths of young Bobby and Richie. *Petersen Foundation collection*

Wishing you Joy & Happiness in 1975.

The Petersens

Bob & Margie, Bobby & Richie

The glowing lioness with her favorite cubs: Margie and the boys. *Petersen Foundation collection*

that Einar was their father's middle name and paternal grandfather's first name. The boys were handsome and smart, and their parents were devoted to them.

But their young lives were cut short, as Gigi Carleton recalls:

The boys had learned to ski the previous winter, and they were so excited about going to Colorado to ski. After arriving in Denver, everyone had to travel beyond in private aircraft, as that's all that could land at the ski resort where they were staying. Bobby and Richie had just made friends with another family with kids their own age, so the boys pleaded with Mr. and Mrs. P. to let them fly in the other plane with them, which they agreed to. Apparently, a sudden snow squall whipped up, and the pilot flying the other family and all the kids was instantly snow blinded in total white-out conditions. They flew into the side of a mountain, and everyone aboard was killed instantly. It was December 26, 1975, the day after Christmas. Bobby was going on eleven, and Richie was nine. We buried them on New Year's Eve day.

It was a catastrophe from which the Petersens never fully recovered. They never discussed the tragedy, publicly or in interviews, though this part of their story may explain why the Petersens were so generous in supporting children's charities.

THE BOYS AND GIRLS CLUB OF HOLLYWOOD

Robert Petersen had never joined the Boy Scouts because he couldn't afford an official shirt. He saw an opportunity to make up for this as an adult when, at the age of thirty, some friends who were active in the Boys & Girls Club of Hollywood asked him to serve on the group's board of directors. Members of the club didn't have to buy a shirt; they could wear anything, and the annual dues were nominal, about five dollars.

By the time of their marriage in January 1963, Mr. Petersen had been involved with the club for years. He saw a chance to include his wife in this pursuit and asked her to chair the organization's first Sweetheart Ball fundraiser. Margie's career in modeling and acting had given her no experience in managing a charitable event, but, with the help of her natural intelligence and others' support, she carried it off successfully.

The Sweetheart Ball was held for several years. Once, in the mid-1960s, the group honored Debbie Reynolds, who was a major Hollywood star. After that event, whenever Mr. Petersen wanted a carmaker (usually a US brand) to donate a car for a charitable cause, Ms. Reynolds would offer to entertain at the donor's annual sales meetings in Detroit for free. (Such donations usually benefitted the Thalians, a charitable organization founded by Petersen and several Hollywood stars.)

The Boys Club of Hollywood also had a camp in the mountain resort community of Running Springs, California, and Petersen donated the money to build an Olympic-size pool there. As part of their ongoing commitment and support for the Boys Club, the Petersens annually sent a large group of campers to the camp free of charge. They frequently went to the Boys Club to see the happy campers off in their bus. Eventually, Mr. Petersen was talked into joining the Boys Clubs National Board of Governors by his friend, "Mr. STP," Andy Granatelli.

The Petersens gave often and deeply when it came to children's charities, such as at this Boys and Girls Club of Los Angeles gathering. They were generous, giving people and, since they had lost their own children, this activity may have helped heal a certain void in their hearts.
Petersen Foundation Trust

The Boys Club of Hollywood ultimately became the Boys & Girls Club of Hollywood (each club is independent from others in their community or city), and the Petersens were active in raising funds for this expanded organization.

In the late 1990s, Mr. Petersen gave the group the deed to the 6725 Sunset Boulevard building that he owned in Hollywood; the organization sold it and bought another Hollywood building that better suited its needs. Today, the group's headquarters is named the Margie & Robert E. Petersen Boys & Girls Club of Hollywood. In 2016, in honor of Bobby and Richie Petersen, the Margie & Robert E. Petersen Foundation donated the funds to rebuild the gymnasium, which is now known as the Bobby & Richie Petersen Gymnasium.

THE 1984 LOS ANGELES OLYMPICS

Gigi Carleton recalls the story of how the Petersens got involved in the 1984 Olympics:

1984 Los Angeles Olympics President and chief organizer Peter Ueberroth originally asked Mr. Petersen to be his shooting sports commissioner, but Mr. Petersen turned him down since he was so busy running his 36-magazine publishing empire. Mr. Ueberroth picked someone else who didn't know very much about shooting sports, let alone turning a vacant dairy farm in Chino, California (about 30 miles east of Los Angeles), into a brand-new shooting sports venue. On a second try, Mr. Ueberroth pleaded with Mr. Petersen to take on the challenge as commissioner, and ultimately Mr. Petersen said yes. This was in November 1983 and, because Mr. P. published Guns & Ammo, Hunting, *and a host of other arms-related titles, he knew what had to be done to create a skeet and trap range, an air rifle building, and pistol and rifle ranges.*

The 1984 Olympic Torch given to Mr. Petersen in recognition of his efforts as shooting sports commissioner for the Los Angeles Games. *Author photo*

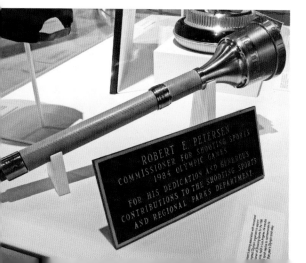

ROBERT E. PETERSEN
COMMISSIONER FOR SHOOTING SPORTS
1984 OLYMPIC GAMES
FOR HIS DEDICATION AND GENEROUS
CONTRIBUTIONS TO THE SHOOTING SPORTS
AND REGIONAL PARKS DEPARTMENT.

Talk about legends, heroes, and friends: check out this impressive lineup taken at the Long Beach Grand Prix in 1976. From left is multiple F1 champion Jack Brabham, Goodyear Racing Tire Executive Leo Mehl, actor/racer James Garner, and Robert E. Petersen. *Petersen Foundation collection*

BELOW: The Petersens were close with the George Barris, "King of the Kustomizers." In the early days of *Hot Rod*, it wasn't unusual for Barris to work as a freelance writer and photographer, shooting and authoring features on the newest custom car creations (his own or those built by others). Here, Barris and Mr. P. check out the '53 Cadillac convertible customized for the ever-flamboyant pianist and entertainer Liberace. *Petersen Photo Archive/TEN: The Enthusiast Network*

OPPOSITE: A great shot from the early days of Bonneville, showing the Hollywood connection goes way back. The gent at left is unidentified, then R. E. P., Wally Parks, and singing cowboy/actor Roy Rogers. *Petersen Photo Archive/ TEN: The Enthusiast Network*

Many of the PPC gun magazine staffers, including editors Ken Elliott and Tom Siatos, were charged with working with the 1984 Olympic Committee to build a first-class Olympic venue in just five months, which was unheard of. Before the venue could be an official site, we had to prove its suitability (by hosting an international shooting competition in April 1984), that all the systems worked, safety requirements were met, and that the property was worthy of being an Olympic venue. Olympic shooting sports medals were the first given to the winning athletes and their countries.

There was no time to waste in getting this venue ready, up and running, especially during a wet and muddy winter. There was no running water or electricity at the site, so it was a big challenge. The International Competition in April 1984 was approved and was the first Olympic venue to open in July 1984. The Olympic committee did not think that shooting sports were going to be very popular and printed only a limited number of tickets. To everyone's surprise, they ran out of tickets on the first day.

ABOVE: The Petersens with Barris's ZZR wild twin-engine custom show rod at Motorama in 1976. *Petersen Photo Archive/TEN: The Enthusiast Network*

RIGHT: Mr. and Mrs. Petersen mugging it up with Barris's most famous custom, the original Batmobile, shot here on the Batcave set for Batman. *Petersen Photo Archive/TEN: The Enthusiast Network*

When Gigi and the Petersens drove into the venue early on the morning of the first day, there was a huge line of people, some with dogs and baby strollers, and little children with their parents, mostly locals—everyone wanted to say they had been to the Olympics. Gigi called one of the company secretaries at the 8490 Sunset Boulevard office and told her to go to a large party store nearby and buy up all the two-stub raffle tickets they had; these became the event's tickets for the next few days.

The venue looked like Camelot, with international flags flying all over the fields. Mrs. Petersen was in charge of the VIP hospitality (commonly known as the Olympic Family Hospitality area), and she and Mr. P. arranged to have Scandia restaurant cater lunch every day. As Gigi recalls, there was no running water

ABOVE: Tough-guy actor Robert Stack was a committed car guy and a longtime friend of the Petersens. He bought this Mercedes-Benz 300SL Gullwing coupe new in the mid-1950s and owned it until his passing. *Petersen Foundation collection*

LEFT: Given their interest in fine food, dining, and entertainment—plus their ownership of the Scandia restaurant—it's no surprise that the Petersens would mingle with a young, up-and-coming celebrity chef named Wolfgang Puck. *Petersen Foundation collection*

New Concept in TV for Youth

Hollywood Citizen-News Saturday, January 24, 1970

Petersen Hits Mark With 'Something Else'

By ALLEN RICH
Television Editor

A rather imposing building on the Sunset Strip bears the title Petersen Publications.

All seven floors of the $2 million structure are given over to the business of producing the company's magazines such as Teen, Hot Rod, Surfing, Motor Trend, Rod and Custom, Skin Diver, etc. and etc.

The full roster of Petersen publications, including an additional variety of books in hard and soft cover, reaches an astronomical readership of more than 25 million a month. Advertising revenue hit a record high of $10.1 million in 1968, but topped even that figure by several millions of dollars in 1969.

The only portion of the large building not utilized by the company is a Bank of America branch on the ground floor. (That makes it handy for the ultra-successful publishing concern!)

month or so and will eventually screen in as many as 175 markets.

They ran the film for me in the Petersen projection room area, an area incidentally comprised of two rooms the decor of which escaped me. I guess you could call it a sort of dimly-lit deep red, Chinese, "antique-moderne" and it provides quite a contrast to the work-a-day adjoining offices with their miniskirted Petersen Co. chicks. It compares oddly, if favorably, with any network projection room I've ever seen.

But to get back to the screening.

Before the man "pushed the button" starting the film, producer Robert Dellinger told me, quote, "It is a difficult task to make contemporary music palatable to a wide age gap. 'Old' folks over 30 tune it out. They don't listen. It's too loud, too much, they think. Consequently, they're missing a lot."

Inasmuch as I am a few hundred years past 10 I guess

sparked by the dancers, with great charm and style. The songs didn't jar you. I don't think I related very well to Three Dog Night, but then who am I to argue with my juniors and the charts?

"Something Else" is an opulent production.

Producer Dellinger explained that each of the 30-minute episodes is budgeted at over $50,000, a very high figure for syndicated programs, most of which come in at about half that.

"Networks thus far have only engaged in tokenism in presenting series for young people. You need look no further than "Music Scene" and "The New People," two of this season's failures, to realize that.

"Our show gives LOCAL stations around the nation another choice than that offered by networks, yet it is of network caliber and I think you'll admit far better than most of its type. It's a pioneering effort in this field.

"Another advantage is that

ABOVE: Mr. P. also dabbled in television and film production. This great newspaper clip talks about a show he produced and launched in 1970 called Something Else, starring actor/comedian John Byner and an ensemble cast. *Petersen Foundation collection*

RIGHT: The incomparable Linda Vaughn would have been a famous personality even if she hadn't appeared in Petersen Publishing magazines over the years. A close friend of the Petersens, here is Miss Hurst Golden Shifter with Mr. P. at his induction into the SEMA Hall of Fame. *Petersen Photo Archive/TEN: The Enthusiast Network*

except for a hose, and no electricity other than portable generators. Once the word was out that the Scandia was serving gourmet lunches in the Olympic family tent, the kings of Sweden and Spain, among other royalty, celebrities, and all the Olympic organizing committee VIPs, all came for lunch.

"This was very gratifying to have such recognition for our shooting sports venue," Gigi remembers. "To the surprise of the Olympic organizing committee we made money and had a very successful event."

LEGENDS, HEROES, AND FRIENDS

It should be clear from these stories that, in Los Angeles, Mr. and Mrs. P. were quite the couple about town. We could easily fill another book with society page press clippings and grip-and-grin photos of this glamorous husband and wife who seemed to know everyone—Hollywood types, musicians, politicians, authors and other publishers, racing drivers, car builders, business and car company executives.

ABOVE: Mr. and Mrs. P. were committed wine enthusiasts and collectors. Here they are at a Confrérie de la Chaîne des Rôtisseurs event in 1992. The gold medal, chain, and green ribbon around his neck indicate that he was then serving as the grand bailli (chapter president) of this organization. *Petersen Foundation collection*

LEFT: Mr. Petersen, left, and Petersen Automotive Museum Executive Director Emeritus Richard G. Messer with the Italian Ghia-bodied 1953 Cadillac once owned by Rita Hayworth, preparing to drive this one-of-two example of Italo-American design in the Pebble Beach Tour d'Elegance. The car completed the seventy-five-mile tour route in comfort and fine style. *Petersen Foundation collection*

Many of these folks were close personal friends, others perhaps less close, but many served with Mr. P. on various boards of directors, in business and for charity organizations. More than a few of them (including Garner, Aldrin, and McQueen) qualify in the "celebrity and car guy friends" category.

The Petersens were around celebrity all of their lives. They respected their many friends for their talents and influence, but they weren't bedazzled by celebrity status alone. They were friends first and had the celeb connections second. That said, when they needed to add a little star power to a party or charity event, they never hesitated to ask these folks to help out, and willingly help they did.

Mr. Petersen was often a guest and honorary judge at the Pebble Beach Concours d'Elegance. Here he is with racing legend Sir Stirling Moss, also an honorary judge, as they prepare to score this exquisite Duesenberg. *Petersen Foundation collection*

From left, Robert E. Petersen, Carroll Shelby, and comedian/actor/racer/car guy Tim Allen at one of the Petersen Museum's annual fundraising galas. Allen has owned many famous hot rods, and he's also made a name for himself as a credible professional racing driver. Shelby needs no further introduction. *Petersen Trust collection*

FAMOUS FRIENDS

Here's just a brief list of some of the local "talent" the Petersens knew as personal friends: Debbie Reynolds, Danny Thomas, James Garner, Charlton Heston, Hugh Hefner, Tom Selleck, Donald O'Connor, Ruta Lee, Connie Stevens, Hugh O'Brian, Roy Rogers, Jack LaLanne, Buzz Aldrin, Richard Anderson, Ernie Borgnine, Larry Hagman, Ruth Buzzi, Herb Shriner (Mr. P.'s best man at his wedding), Rhonda Fleming, Jack Carter, Carol Channing, Phyllis Diller, Gary Collins, Mary Ann Mobley, Erik Estrada, John Frankenheimer, Mona Freeman, Constance Towers, Mitzi Gaynor, Mary Hart, Tippi Hedren, Florence Henderson, Anne Jeffreys, Peter Marshall, Terry Moore, Rip Taylor, Dick Van Patten, Lyle Waggoner, Jerry Weintraub, David Wolper, Jo Anne Worley, and Steve McQueen.

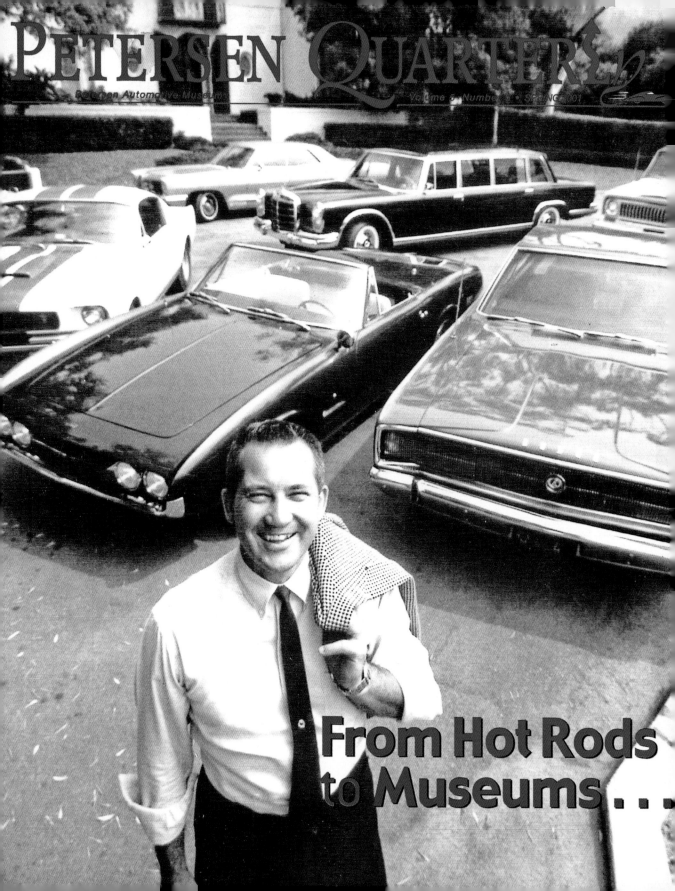

PETERSEN QUARTERLY

Petersen Automotive Museum · Volume 6 · Number 1 · SPRING 2001

From Hot Rods to Museums . . .

6

The Petersen Automotive Museum—
The Final Gem in the Petersen Crown

··

The Hollywood Motorama Museum didn't fulfill the high expectations the Petersens had for the venture, and the venue closed after only a decade. They still believed that Los Angeles, one of the most important centers of automotive culture, society, style, and sport, would support a world-class

··

automotive museum. Their ideas for such a museum were well defined from the beginning: it would celebrate automotive history, culture, and technology; it would be somewhat like the Motorama Museum, but larger, grander, and more developed; it would feature cars used in film and on television, including those that were prominent in pop culture; and it would serve as an educational entity to help teach and inspire young people.

Not far from where Petersen helped stage that first Hot Rod Expo in 1948 stood the Natural History Museum of Los Angeles County, located in Exposition Park in downtown L.A. The museum had a strong collection of interesting cars, mostly those important in California history, and many produced in Los Angeles or around Southern California. Some of these were displayed occasionally, but most were locked away in the museum's storage buildings, literally and metaphorically gathering dust. Petersen

OPPOSITE: Another famous Petersen driveway photo of Mr. P. with some of his cars. The Ghia 450SS still belongs to the museum, but the Mercedes-Benz 600 was sold off. We're not sure of the current ownership status of the Shelby GT350, Charger, Jeep, or Pontiac also seen in this photo. *Petersen Automotive Museum photo, courtesy Kahn Media*

felt the Natural History Museum could be a valuable partner in creating a new automotive museum for Los Angeles. The natural history folks knew the museum business, in addition to understanding the political and legal issues involved in managing an automotive museum. Additionally, their basement was full of significant, interesting cars.

The Petersens knew their way around the Los Angeles property game. Their idea was to source and provide a venue for the new automotive museum, which the Natural History Museum would curate and operate. Once approached by

ABOVE: When the old department store building was remodeled into the first iteration of the Petersen Automotive Museum, it looked particularly dazzling at night. Those steel spires did a lot to make the building look taller and pop out from the surrounding streetscape. *Petersen Automotive Museum photo, courtesy Kahn Media*

LEFT: The Petersen Automotive Museum's original grand opening was grand indeed. Here, James Garner, California Governor Pete Wilson, and Mr. and Mrs. P. cut the ceremonial ribbon. *Petersen Foundation collection*

the Petersens, the museum leadership agreed that everyone would benefit from the arrangement. The property would bear the name of its founding benefactors, Margie and Robert E. Petersen, and become the Petersen Automotive Museum (PAM). The museum administrators started arranging financing, and the Petersens began hunting for the ideal location.

They didn't have to look far. Recall that the Petersens' office was located at 6420 Wilshire Boulevard. Just half a mile to the east, at the western edge of the Los Angeles Museum District, sat a vacant building that seemed ideal for the new museum.

Ohrbach's department store at 6060 Wilshire Boulevard was one of those old-school "boulevard" retailers common in Los Angeles. With a Streamline Moderne jewel, the May Company Building, on Wilshire Boulevard just across the street and the art deco Bullocks Wilshire a few miles to the east, the location had some architecturally impressive neighbors. Orbach's operated in the three-story building from 1965 until it went out of business in 1986. When the Petersens found it, the building wasn't derelict, but it was vacant and for sale. They thought it was just the right size for the new Petersen Automotive Museum, so they bought the

Even in the less glamorous light of day, the Petersen Museum was a big statement for a big Los Angeles corner. It stood a short walk from PPC's headquarters, and Mr. and Mrs. P. visited a lot. *Petersen Automotive Museum photo, courtesy Kahn Media*

property in 1992 as their donation to the project. According to the plan, the new museum should be ready to open by mid-1994.

The property wasn't perfect, but it had a lot going for it, primarily its prominent location within the Wilshire Boulevard Museum District. A handsome enough property as they found it, the architectural redesign called for massive iron spires intended to make the building look more interesting, less boxy. The underground warehouse provided spaces for a small shop and storage to house collection cars that were not being displayed. Most importantly, the property had a multilevel parking structure for the public and a large, uncovered upper parking deck that was the perfect spot for outdoor car events and overflow parking when needed. Getting the building fully redesigned, retrofitted, decorated, and filled in a year and a half was an aggressive undertaking, but the Petersens and the Natural History Museum team were fully committed to getting the job done on time for a June 1994 grand opening. And so they did.

OPPOSITE TOP: The museum's original design for the ground floor was intended to be a stroll through automotive history and culture, presented as a sequence of dioramas. *Petersen Automotive Museum photo, courtesy Kahn Media*

OPPOSITE BOTTOM: This exceptionally rare custom Touring-bodied Ferrari Barchetta helped inspire the original 1955 Ford Thunderbird. It was a gift from Enzo Ferrari to the Ford family in the early 1950s. *Author photo*

BELOW: The "Suburban Garage" diorama could be dressed to suit the period of the car parked there. This is a 1963 Studebaker Wagonaire, and the garage is filled with the usual paraphernalia of the day: ice chests, tennis rackets, a Ping-Pong table, bumper stickers, tools, and all the other things you'd expect. Cute! *Author photo*

Everyone's favorite car guy, Jay Leno, is a frequent guest of the Petersen Automotive Museum. He has emceed many events there. *Author photo*

The interior design, layout, and exhibit structures represented a major step forward from the Motorama Museum. The basement, quickly nicknamed "the Vault," remained the primary storage area for collection cars not on display. The new first-floor entrance and gift shop were reoriented to face the interior of the parking structure. The first floor was almost entirely filled with diorama-style exhibits illustrating scenes that included early motoring in Los Angeles, a diner, a hot dog stand, a speed shop, a fuel station, an elegant 1930s-era new car showroom, a typical suburban two-car garage, automotive design studio, and a hot rod shop. Although guests were free to view the exhibits in any order they wished, the dioramas were designed to follow a path through history; some were fixed, meaning their cars remained a permanent part of the display, while others changed and evolved. These changing showrooms could be dressed up as a Duesenberg salon, a Cadillac dealership, or whatever the curators deemed interesting or appropriate at the moment; sometimes the theme was determined by major exhibits featured elsewhere in the museum.

The second floor was intended to host revolving and evolving exhibits that changed every six months or so. The various galleries were named after many of the museum's board members and most significant donors, including Bruce Meyer and *L.A. Times* Publisher Otis Chandler. Many innovative exhibits have been staged here, including one dedicated to low riders, an automotive style and culture that was born in nearby Whittier, California, in the early 1970s. One of the museum's galleries was dedicated to exhibits featuring motorcycles. In 1997, to celebrate Ferrari's fiftieth

ABOVE AND LEFT: Carroll Shelby and Mr. Petersen had been friends and business associates for fifty years, so there was little question that Shelby's memorial celebration in 2012 would be held at the museum. Hundreds of Shelby cars (including Cobras, Mustangs, and Shelby Chryslers) are on display at PAM. *Author photos*

anniversary, the Ferrari factory and family sponsored a large, lavish display of Ferrari models from the company's considerable history.

The third floor served as a multipurpose space, housing the museum staff's offices and several areas dedicated to children's education and exhibits. On the rooftop, the William E. Connor Penthouse is a glass-walled, rectangular room that hosts elegant events, dinners, and meetings. The glass-and-steel-beamed structure takes perfect advantage of the building's spectacular views of the Hollywood Hills and Los Angeles city skyline.

As it was realized following its 1994 opening, the Petersen Automotive Museum was a dazzling, fun, and informative place. All of the stakeholders who contributed—the Petersens, the Natural History Museum system, and the city of Los Angeles—were justifiably proud of what they had helped create.

The cars housed and exhibited in the Petersen Automotive Museum fall into a variety of categories. One group could be called the permanent collection, including cars previously owned by the Natural History Museum and those that have been acquired or donated since the PAM's founding. The museum also features cars or collections borrowed on long-term loan for specific exhibits. When the museum hosted the Ferrari anniversary exhibit, most of the cars displayed were privately owned, although a rare few did belong to the museum itself. The Petersens were another source of museum and exhibit cars: they often donated cars and motorcycles purchased specifically for the museum's permanent collection, in addition to many cars from their personal collection that they gave to the museum.

The museum's annual fundraising gala is always a star-studded affair. In the past it has been hosted by Jay Leno, James Corden, and other big names from the entertainment industry. When Carroll Shelby passed away in 2012, the museum hosted a memorial celebration in his honor, with the rooftop positively flooded with Shelby Cobras and Mustangs. Many television specials and movie scenes have been filmed at the museum, and the property is often the site of fashion and car magazine photo shoots. Several collector car auctions have been staged sales there as well.

The museum has even earned a footnote in a celebrity murder case. Christopher George Latore Wallace, AKA The Notorious B.I.G., attended a Soul Train music awards after-party at the Petersen on March 8, 1997. Shortly after the controversial rapper left the party in his car, just after midnight on March 9, he was gunned down nearby on Wilshire Boulevard in a drive-by shooting.

The museum operated and many would say thrived under its generally workable, but hardly ideal organizational scenario. The museum was always solvent, but seldom profitable enough to undertake some of the major property and physical plant improvements the board of directors felt were needed. Revenue from sponsorships, donations, and event fees could not fund all of these projects. It seems the financial approach under which the museum was initially funded was unrealistic in terms of visitor attendance projections and admission income. And some hoped-for car purchases and restorations couldn't be funded.

Executive Director Emeritus Richard G. Messer once said that "the 'bone people' from the Natural History Museum system may understand dinosaurs, but they don't know much about cars." The Petersens were frustrated at having to go to the Natural History Museum board to ask for permission or funding every time they wanted to undertake various projects.

So the Petersens stepped up in a big way to establish the museum's independence and ensure without question its financial and operational future. At what price freedom? In this case, $25 million.

In April of 2000, the Petersens stroked out a check for that amount to pay off the bond debt used to finance the original project. This also established the Petersen Automotive Museum Foundation as an independent, nonprofit entity, no longer under the control of the Natural History Museum organization. Now free of that debt service and the oversight of its former managers, the museum became instantly more profitable—and financially sustainable. More importantly, it had more freedom to buy, sell, restore, and manage its collection as it saw fit.

A year after the museum foundation was established, its leadership began contemplating an expansion of the building, to bring the museum up to date. They announced their goal of raising $50 million to fund the project. Various concepts were considered over the next decade, until 2013, when an ambitious plan to reinvent the museum was finalized. Plans were made to close the property for a one-year rebuild and refit, initially estimated to cost around $95 million. The fundraising drive was led by Museum Chairman Peter Mullin,

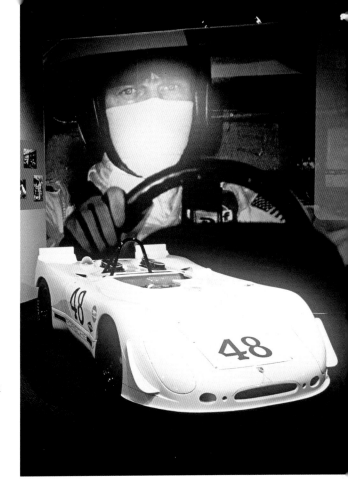

ABOVE AND OPPOSITE: One of the museum's most popular exhibits was dedicated to the automotive life of Steve McQueen. It was a landmark gathering of McQueen's cars, bikes, and personal effects; the exhibit highlighted the famous motorcycle jump stunt from The Great Escape, as well as some of McQueen's off-road motorcycles; in this case, we're looking at a Husqvarna and two Triumphs. The white racing car is the Porsche 908 in which McQueen and Peter Revson finished second overall in the 1970 12 Hours of Sebring endurance race. *Author photos*

RIGHT: An impressive gathering of Bonneville racers and friends at the museum. From left, ABC radio talk show host "Motorman" Leon Kaplan, Bruce Meyer, Robert E. Petersen, Margie Petersen, land-speed-record-holder Craig Breedlove, Alex Xydias, and Wally Parks. *Petersen Foundation collection*

BELOW: The dynamic visage of the "new" Petersen Automotive Museum is dazzlingly unique, a bold architectural statement in Los Angeles. The red steel framework and stainless-steel bands look like different things to different eyes, but they're certainly like nothing else in the world. The structure positively glows in this dusk light. *Petersen Automotive Museum photo, courtesy Kahn Media*

Chairman Emeritus Bruce Meyer, and board member David Sydorick, among other noted big-time car collectors. The project's goal was to entirely reimagine the property, its mission, its interior and exterior design aesthetics, and use of technology and space. The Petersens contributed a great deal, and there were also substantial corporate and private donations, sponsorships, and partnerships that helped raise the money. The Petersen Automotive Museum closed for a major facelift in October 2014.

The plan was challenging: how could the museum make better use of its existing space without moving or removing structural exterior walls, and without compromising the much-needed parking space, since there was no additional vacant property for expansion? The museum's curators, collection managers, and exhibit designers were joined by a team of outside experts to ensure that the needed expertise was available to achieve their

ABOVE: The corner of Wilshire and Fairfax has been home to several examples of unique architecture. Directly across the street to the north is the May Company Building, a former department store built in the Streamline Moderne style in 1939; having served as an annex for the Los Angeles Museum of Contemporary Art (LACMA) since 1994, it is currently being expanded and remodeled into the new Academy Museum of Motion Pictures. The Petersen stands in good company at the western edge of L.A.'s Museum Row. *Petersen Automotive Museum photo, courtesy Kahn Media*

LEFT: This rooftop shot shows some of the structural elements of the museum's red-ribbon-and-steel exterior, with the glass-walled Rooftop Penthouse & Terrace, a banquet and meeting room, just to the right. *Author photo*

BELOW LEFT: The street-level view on Fairfax Avenue allows visitors to get close to the metal sculpture that gives the museum its new look. It's sure to be the backdrop for countless Facebook and Instagram posts in coming years. *Author photo*

goals. These experts included architects Kohn Pedersen Fox Associates, MATT Construction, A. Zahner Company (for design, construction, engineering and metal fabrication), and The Scenic Route (for exhibit design and construction). This marvelous confluence of talent set out to turn the Petersen Automotive Museum into a "Guggenheim for cars."

We asked Gene Kohn, principle architect of Kohn Pedersen Fox, what inspired the museum's new visage of sweeping red- and steel-colored bands that now drape the building, once described as a combination of a "roller coaster track, flames painted on the grille and hood of a hot rod, and a red-headed woman's hair blowing in the wind while riding in an open roadster." Kohn said the basic premise of the concept was to "ensure the reinvented Petersen Automotive Museum looked like nothing else, and would be unique in all the world."

Think about it: when you see the Empire State Building, the Golden Gate Bridge, and the Eiffel Tower, you know what they are, and where they are. They are unmistakable design statements. Los Angeles has some of them, like the Capitol Records building in Hollywood, the Broad Museum of Modern Art, and the Disney Concert Hall. We wanted the new Petersen to join lists of unmistakable landmarks like these. Some people will love it, others are free to hate it, but anyone seeing the building or a photo of it will know exactly what and where it is.

We mentioned that some of the red tubular girders reach right down to street level, and are unfenced and otherwise unprotected from

ABOVE: The Scenic Route Company designed and created this massive spiral grand staircase, which is without question the most romantic and visually exciting way to move from floor to floor in the new Petersen. It is wheelchair friendly, but there's an elevator if you prefer. *Author photo*

OPPOSITE TOP LEFT: That's Elvis Presley's yellow De Tomaso Pantera on the left, and, if you look just beyond, you'll see the Magnum PI Ferrari 308 GTS and the Breaking Bad Pontiac Aztek. *Author photo*

OPPOSITE TOP RIGHT: At left is the latest car driven by Bond, James Bond—an Aston Martin DB10— and the Jaguar on the right is a concept car design tapped as the Bond villain's ride in the 007 film Spectre. *Author photo*

ABOVE: You can't get more vintage California than a '56 Chevrolet Bel Air convertible. This is what welcomed you to the upper floors at the time of the museum's grand reopening. Note the black ceilings, sharply focused lighting, and highly polished concrete floors. *Author photo*

TOP: Three of the world's most iconic hot rod custom cars appear together at the Petersen. The black roadster is the renowned Doane Spencer Deuce. A noted California hot rodder, designer, racer, and fabricator, Spencer distilled many custom touches into this seminal '32 Ford Roadster hot rod, then hand-built it himself. Bruce Meyer owns it now. It's been shown and has won awards at Pebble Beach, and now it spends a lot of time at the museum. *Author photo*

passersby, to which Kohn replied, "Oh, that was on purpose—we want visitors to see how it's built, get close with the architecture, and line up next to it for their vacation photos and selfies." Inspired thinking, for sure.

The museum's executive director, Terry Karges, was equally pleased and inspired by his new baby, commenting:

I am proud to announce that the new Petersen Automotive Museum is open on schedule [December 7, 2015], on budget and with interior and exterior designs that are even more stunning then the concept renderings—and that is a rare feat in both the architecture and museum worlds. Thanks to the efforts of Kohn Pedersen Fox, MATT Construction, A. Zahner Company, The Scenic Route, and our incredible Petersen team, we have transformed a building that was once an old department store into one of the most groundbreaking structures in Los Angeles. What's inside is just as stunning, including a three-story spiral staircase that transports visitors through 25 galleries representing the history, industry and artistry of the automobile.

OPPOSITE BOTTOM LEFT: "*Hot Rod 1*" could only be Robert E. Petersen. The museum proudly displays a gallery of its founding benefactor's personal affects in the Hot Rod Gallery. *Author photo*

OPPOSITE BOTTOM MIDDLE The Petersen personal effects gallery also contains property from Mr. P.'s other magazine titles and his various personal and business ventures, such as this Petersen Aviation baseball cap. *Author photo*

OPPOSITE BOTTOM RIGHT: The iconic "golden caliper" *Motor Trend* Car of the Year trophy, presented by the *Motor Trend* staff to Mr. and Mrs. Petersen on the occasion of *Motor Trend's* fiftieth anniversary. *Author photo*

BELOW: The Peter and Merle Mullin Artistry Floor is all about miles of style, embodied the art of the automobile. From left: grand, classic examples of Rolls-Royce, Bentley, Bugatti, Mercedes-Benz, and Delahaye. Magnificent! *Author photo*

The Alexander Calder BMW 3.0 CSL Art Car is no staid canvas: it actually raced in this livery. *Author photo*

The new Petersen Automotive Museum now has three full floors, with 95,000 square feet of exhibit space—an increase of about 15,000 square feet without moving a single exterior wall. One architectural element that proved effective was the relocation of all the office space from the third floor to the basement. That basement office space was designed and equipped with special "eye-friendly" lighting and other environmental measures to ensure the staff didn't feel like they were, literally or figuratively, locked in the basement. The spaces are comfortable, attractive, and finished in themes, color, and materials that tie them directly to the exhibit space.

As charming as they were, the old diorama-style exhibits are gone. The new third floor is designated "History," a nostalgic place to dive into the exhibit space proper, with a multifaceted look at the history of the automobile, "where society meets invention and technology." One exhibit at the time of the reopening focused on concept cars as art, showing what the future looked like from the perspective of the 1950s and 1960s. Informed by the Petersens' pop cultural awareness, the Hollywood Gallery includes a Batmobile, the *Magnum P.I.* Ferrari 308 that was driven on-screen by Tom Selleck, the Pontiac Aztek from *Breaking Bad*, and two great movie cars from the James Bond thriller *Spectre*: the villain's mid-engined Jaguar exotic hyper car and 007's fabulous Aston Martin DB10. The Automobile Club of Southern California also presents "Southern California: A Region in Motion," which uses interactive video content to demonstrate how, unlike other major cities, Los Angeles "grew out" instead of "up."

ABOVE: The new Petersen's museum store stocks modestly priced items, but it also serves as an automotive boutique that transcends the typical "end-of-the-tour gift shop." The store offers high-quality books, wearables, models, and artwork. *Petersen Automotive Museum photo, courtesy Kahn Media*

LEFT: You won't starve at the Petersen Automotive Museum. While vending machines serving up microwaved hot dogs are absent, the decidedly Italian Drago Brothers run their namesake *ristorante* onsite, open to the public with or without a museum ticket. *Author photo*

What treasures of the Vault hide beneath those Covercraft car covers? All kinds of greatness, in this case a Toyota 2000GT and a DeLorean DMC-12, foreground. *Evan Klein photo*

Proceeding to the second floor, we say "forget the elevator and take the grand staircase" to the floor featuring permanent and changing exhibits. One gallery, aptly named the *Hot Rod* Gallery, is dedicated to California car culture, hot rodding, and the Petersens. It includes a display case full of Mr. Petersen's personal effects, including one of his cameras, his typewriter, his *Hot Rod* #1 jacket, hats, and a variety of automotive-related trophies, plaques, and awards he received during his life. Another exhibit keeps the museum family-friendly: kids can enjoy devices and displays that star characters from the Pixar movie *Cars*. This floor features vehicles powered by alternative fuels, illustrating the future—or the fantasy—of powertrain development technology. There are solar-powered cars, pure electrics, steam-powered cars, even a few that burn coal. Texas oilman and serious vintage racing car collector driver Charles Nearburg sponsored the Nearburg Family Gallery, which features cars as well as an impressive theater in the half-round dedicated to motorsports. The second floor also contains a large open gallery space dedicated to motorcycles, motorcycle racing, and scooters. There's something for everyone on this floor.

Follow the grand staircase down to the ground level, where the Peter and Merle Mullin Artistry Floor is dedicated to grand classics and cars as art. The Mullins shared with the Petersens a love of classic-era 1920s and 1930s cars with elegant custom coachwork; on this floor, you'll find a vast display of the finest coachwork-era machines from Bugatti, Delage, Delahaye, Talbot-Lago, and other such uber-collectible marques. The flavor of this floor is definitely art deco, based on the style of these great, primarily European marques. Continuing the themes of cars as art, the Armand Hammer Foundation Gallery has hosted a variety of work inspired and created by some of the world's finest modern artists. This gallery has displayed most of the "BMW Art Cars" designed and painted by notables such as Alexander Calder, David Hockney, and Andy Warhol.

The new PAM also has a gift and book shop with toys for kids and lots of high-quality books and magazines, models and collectibles, and wearables for enthusiasts of all tastes. And speaking of tastes, you'll likely end your visit hungry. Fortunately, the Drago Brothers can address that need with their Drago Ristorante on the first floor. These Italian brothers, owners of many fine restaurants and a world-class catering business in Southern California, operate this casually elegant Italian restaurant right

This elegant 1937 Delage D8 coupe was among Mrs. Petersen's favorite cars. She told me she loved the curvaceous French coachwork and the understated gold-and-maroon paint scheme. Author photo

TOP: Katherine Hepburn had style for days, and so does her triple black '66 Chrysler Imperial convertible. This one is a part of the museum's permanent collection, in excellent, highly original condition. *Author photo*

inside the museum. Patrons can enjoy a glass of wine along with a fresh Italian appetizer, main dish, or pizza after your walk through automotive history. Yum.

Finally, take a tour of the Vault. Before the museum's remodeling and reopening, the Vault wasn't open to the public. Everyone loves a look behind the curtain or into Aladdin's cave when given the chance. Now you can schedule your docent-led Vault tour when you purchase regular entry tickets, and the upcharge is minimal. The Vault Tour is a truly worthwhile addition to the PAM experience.

The Vault isn't a brightly lit or fastidiously curated exhibit. It's just what it sounds like: a massive, basement-level warehouse full of cars. Most are museum collection cars that aren't currently on display. Each is waiting for its moment to return to the main exhibit floors; many are in line for restoration or other mechanical fettling. The shop area is intended for basic repairs and maintenance, not heavy-duty restoration or mechanical work (though some can be performed here). There's a large area dedicated to shop and parts manuals, a caged-in room for storing spare engines, and rows and rows of cars awaiting their change at exhibition. Some are under cover, some not. You may see Katharine Hepburn's Chrysler Imperial convertible, a George Barris creation, or the Greased Lightning customized Ford driven by John Travolta in *Grease*. The room is wonderful for its authenticity as a big underground barn full of hidden gems—it even smells like old cars.

The museum receives many cars as donations; some are bequeathed to the collection, others are donated primarily for tax benefits. There are numerous rules and regulations regarding such donations, and information about donating a vehicle is available at www.petersen.org or from the museum's curatorial office. Gifting a car to the Petersen can help the museum in several ways. If the car has historical significance, it could end up on display, or it could provide parts or components needed to restore another vehicle in the collection. It may also be sold, at the

BELOW: A big car, literally and metaphorically, this 1972 Mercedes-Benz SWB 600 was once owned by actor Jack Nicholson. He drove it in the film *The Witches of Eastwick* and donated it personally to the museum. *Mel Stone photo*

OPPOSITE BOTTOM: The Vault contains "works in progress" and "ladies in waiting," such as these Muntz Jets, two of the three owned by the museum. The third is an average car restored to driving condition, but the two shown here were California-built examples, one of which has some old Hollywood celebrity provenance. The third Jet will probably be sold to finance the restoration of this pair. *Author photo*

museum's discretion, to help fund the purchase or restoration of other vehicles in the collection. If are interested in donating a vehicle or giving a financial contribution, the PAM staff would love to hear from you.

The Petersens were immensely proud of the museum that bears their name. As we've seen, they contributed many cars to the collection, and they supported and attended events, openings, shows, and galas there. As Executive Director Emeritus Ken Gross put it:

Millions today share a passion for great cars because Robert E. Petersen followed his heart. Thanks to his foresight and generosity—and that of wife Margie— millions more have the opportunity to learn about our unique and exciting automotive heritage . . . at the Petersen Automotive Museum.

LEFT: This brutishly elegant Mercedes-Benz 196 was once raced by five-time F1 driving champion Juan Manuel Fangio. *Author photo*

BELOW: The museum has vastly increased its collection of Steve McQueen–owned cars and bikes with this fabulous foursome: the two motorcycles in the foreground are ex-McQueen Indians, the Hudson is a Wasp coupe he owned late in his life, and the Jaguar is his 1956 XK-SS, nicknamed "The Green Rat." The Petersens purchased all of these vehicles for the museum during their lifetime, and it's safe to say they will remain staple elements of the museum's permanent collection. *Evan Klein photo*

OPPOSITE TOP LEFT: You will not find a happier, handsomer car enthusiast and mega-collector than Robert E. Petersen, here looking quite fine next to this gleaming Rolls-Royce town car. *Petersen Automotive Museum photo, courtesy Kahn Media*

OPPOSITE TOP RIGHT: A smiling Mr. and Mrs. Petersen check on the restoration of their "round-door" 1925 Rolls-Royce Phantom 1 Jonckheere Aerodynamic Coupe. Without question one of the stars of their collection, it now holds a similar status in the museum's permanent collection. *Petersen Automotive Museum photo, courtesy Kahn Media*

OPPOSITE BOTTOM: Few shades of silver are more famous than Aston Martin's Silver Birch, as seen on this appropriately James Bondish DB5 Coupe. *Author photo*

Here are three cars that once belonged to famous car guy (and actor) Clark Gable: his 1941 Cadillac Series 62 Coupe Custom at left, 1949 Jaguar XK-120 in the middle, and 1956 Mercedes-Benz 300 Sc Cabriolet at right. This summit of Gable Greats occurred on the Petersen Museum rooftop. *Author photo*

Epilogue

As the Petersens got older, they began to plan for their later years and retirement. According to *Forbes* magazine, Mr. Petersen had a net worth of $700 million. The couple could have any car they wanted. They'd traveled the world, had built a world-class car museum that bore their name, and, due to the tragic loss of their sons, had no direct heirs. The magazine publishing business was changing: evolving subscription models and the advent of the internet had a direct impact on this industry. In 1996, the Petersens quietly elected to put the company up for sale. Gigi recalls that she and the Petersens traveled to New York for meetings about which, strangely enough, she was given no details. She remembers their driver dropping Mr. Petersen off at a Manhattan office building; he instructed Gigi and Mrs. Petersen to do some shopping or otherwise occupy themselves, telling them he would be done in time to meet them for lunch. In truth, he was heading for a meeting at Goldman Sachs to put the company up for sale. Gigi recalls the spectacular lunch they had after he was done, complemented by more than a little wine and champagne. While they ate, Mr. P. told them what he had done. It was bittersweet for sure, but PPC had been their life and support since 1948, and it was time to move on.

ABOVE: It should come as no surprise that Bobby and Richie Petersen loved cars from the start. *Petersen Foundation collection*

OPPOSITE: Mr. and Mrs. Petersen dress up in their "great white hunter" garb for this couple-at-home photo. Both were outdoorsy types, so this look suited them well. *Petersen Foundation collection*

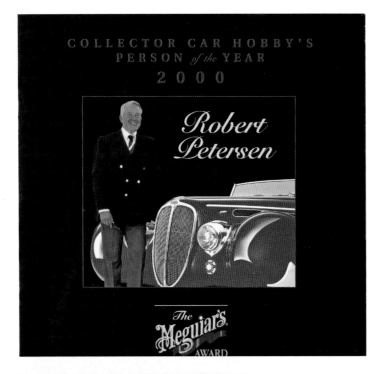

A group of New York investors had purchased the company. They didn't really understand the publishing business, and the general consensus was that they had paid too much for it at the time. The company floundered and languished, but survived. In 1998, two years after Petersen had given up the reins of the company, the owners sold it to a British publishing concern called EMAP. Though experienced in the media game, EMAP never fully got its head around the company and brands, either. The Petersen Publishing Company had grown since its first three decades of existence, and Mr. Petersen had gradually acquired numerous smaller publishing houses and specialty titles. When he sold the company, it was for well over $400 million. EMAP passed the company to Primedia, which participated in selling off portions of the PPC's assets, held additional sales and reorganizations, and implemented at least one "prepackaged" bankruptcy filing that was little more than a reorganization of debt.

TOP LEFT: Mr. Petersen was honored as Meguiar's Collector Car Hobbyist of the Year in 2000, and he was given the prestigious Meguiar's Award in honor of his contributions to the automotive enthusiast community. *Petersen Foundation collection*

LEFT: The relationship between Gigi Carleton and Margie Petersen extended well beyond their roles as employee and employer. They were lifelong friends and constant companions after Mr. Petersen passed away. *Petersen Foundation collection*

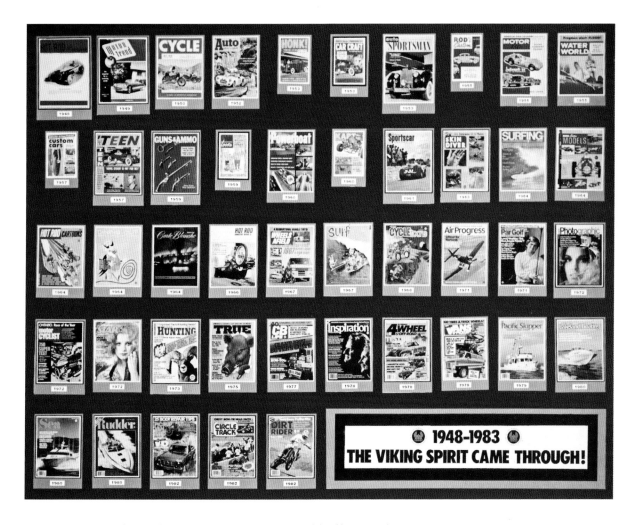

Various titles and magazine groups were sold off, recombining into Source Interlink Media, which today operates as two entities called TEN: The Enthusiast Network Publishing and The Enthusiast Network, a Discovery Communications company. While the latter focuses on television, as well as subscription and online video assets, some of which are tied to magazine titles, TEN Publishing still owns and publishes *Hot Rod*, the retro-themed *Hot Rod Deluxe, Motor Trend, Car Craft*, and a host of other titles launched during the Petersens' tenure.

Once the publishing company was sold, the Petersens continued to dabble in various business interests. They maintained Petersen Properties for their real estate interests, along with the aviation company, a restaurant group, and even some additional publishing ventures. They

Mr. Petersen was justifiably proud of his Viking heritage, here credited for the success of the Petersen Publishing Company. This is what the company's fleet of magazine titles looked like as of 1983. *Petersen Foundation collection*

ABOVE: This staged portrait was a great look for Mr. P., who often mixed a dress shirt and tie with a casual, outdoorsy, or Western jacket. *Petersen Foundation collection*

OPPOSITE TOP: The company regularly published a brochure outlining the "Petersen Story" as an advertising sales piece to familiarize potential clients with the company's origin and history. *Petersen Foundation collection*

OPPOSITE BOTTOM: One of our favorite photos of Mr. Petersen in one of his most natural elements, walking through nature with a shotgun broken open over his shoulders, after a day of hunting or trapshooting. *Petersen Foundation collection*

also kept busy with the Petersen Automotive Museum and the couple's many charity efforts and causes. And they always maintained a relationship with the publishing company, appearing at events or sitting for an occasional interview.

For Gigi Carleton, coming up with one story or memory that really defined Mr. Petersen was difficult and emotional, especially given their near-fifty-year friendship and employment relationship. But she does tell one story that says a lot about the man:

In the early 2000s, Mr. & Mrs. P. and I were driving to an appointment in Topanga Canyon, California. I was at the wheel of his 2002 Cadillac, which was his daily driver. We decided to drive down the Pacific Coast Highway (more scenic than the 101 Freeway). We turned up Topanga Canyon, a two-lane canyon road heading toward the San Fernando Valley. All of sudden, Mr. P. said, "Stop the car, stop the car." I pulled over and couldn't imagine what had happened. He got out of the car and looked down this gully and said, "You won't believe this!" Many years ago, there had been a burglary at his office, and the petty cash and his file box with all the 3x5 cards with the names and addresses of the Hot Rod magazine subscription base were stolen. Somehow, along the way, Mr. P. was told he could find his 3x5 subscriber cards in Topanga Canyon. So way back in the day, in his suit and tie and dress shoes, he searched the canyon and found his 3x5 subscription cards scattered in this particular gully. Long before the advent of computerized mailing lists and labeling, these cards were the lifeblood of the Hot Rod magazine readership, and he gathered them all up. Funny thing is that he remembered the exact location after more than 50 years, so he just wanted to stop, take a look, laugh, and remember the whole somewhat bizarre story.

Robert E. Petersen died March 23, 2007, of neuroendocrine cancer. He was just 80. Naturally, Mrs. Petersen was crushed but soldiered on for several more years, ultimately succumbing to breast cancer on November 25, 2011, at the age of 76. It is a shame of immeasurable proportions that their sons didn't live to carry on and enjoy their legacy, and a further disappointment that Mr. and Mrs. P. didn't live to see the breathtaking reimagination and remodeling of their namesake car museum. I'm confident they would have loved it.

It's impossible to calculate the number of lives the Petersens touched along the way. They published millions of magazines. Their work had a profound impact on professional drag racing and the automotive performance aftermarket. They donated

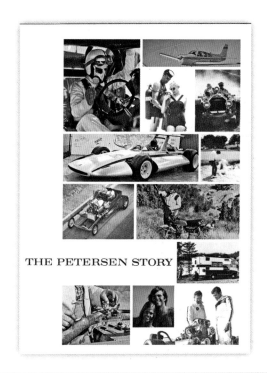

THE PETERSEN STORY

Another great "typical Pete" shot of Mr. P. helping sell magazines at the races out of the Petersen Publishing Company trailer. For a wealthy man who spent a lot of time in a suit or a tuxedo, he was just as happy in a Western-style getup: button-down shirt, jeans, and a bush hat. *Petersen Foundation collection*

millions of dollars to many, many charities. Their guidance and perseverance in developing the Petersen Automotive Museum has brought automotive education and sheer pleasure to all those who have visited what they helped build.

About six months before her death, Mrs. Petersen donated substantial amounts of money to the charities and concerns most important to her, including the hospital where she underwent cancer treatment, as well as to religious organizations and a variety of children's charities. The Petersens had earlier established the Margie & Robert E. Petersen Foundation, and Mrs. Petersen further ensured the future of the couple's namesake automotive museum. In those months before her passing, the museum released the following statement:

LOS ANGELES (April 26, 2011)—Steven E. Young, Chairman of the Petersen Automotive Museum Foundation's Board of Directors, announced today that the Museum Foundation has received a gift of approximately $100,000,000 from Margie Petersen and the Margie & Robert E. Petersen Foundation.

This donation is comprised of a substantial unrestricted financial gift, a matching challenge, the . . . building that the Museum has occupied since it opened in 1994, and an important collection of cars assembled by the late Robert E. Petersen during his lifetime, all as part of the Museum's gift.

This gift ensures that the Museum will continue to grow in importance as one of Los Angeles's premier museums, and the largest and most acclaimed automobile museum in the nation.

"I am thrilled to make this gift which continues what Mr. Petersen and I began two decades ago, to build the most important automotive museum in the nation. My intent in doing this is to provide the Museum with the necessary resources to continue to enhance its collections, curatorial expertise and exhibitions so that

generations to come will be able to forever know the history of the automobile and its role in the evolution of our nation's transportation system," said Margie Petersen.

"I am fulfilling a vision that Mr. Petersen and I shared and planned to do someday. I am so happy that this day has come and that I can launch the Museum into a new era of growth and expansion. While I expect the resources of the Museum to be available to the world, this gift is especially designed to the benefit of the Los Angeles community where we made our lives together," stated Margie Petersen.

A program of special importance to Mrs. Petersen has been the Museum's Free School Bus Program. Since 2005, the Museum has funded transportation that has enabled approximately 8,000 students per year from the Los Angeles Unified School District, grades K through 12, to visit the Museum. Teachers use the automobile to inspire student thinking about science, art, design, engineering, fuel supply, transportation and urban planning. Many teachers have stated that without this program the children would not have the opportunity to explore learning outside the classroom at all during the school year.

"The Petersen Automotive Museum Foundation Board is honored to acknowledge this gift as it launches a campaign to enlarge the Board and expand the reach of the Museum. We are committed to make the Petersen Automotive Museum the most important automobile venue in the world," said Board Chairman Steven Young.

The Petersens' magnificent Beverly Hills home, their considerable wine collection, personal effects, and some of their daily driver cars were sold at an estate sale not long after Mrs. Petersen's passing. Mr. Petersen's world-renowned vintage weaponry and gun collection was donated to the National Rifle Association's museum at the time of his passing, and is now on public display in a special gallery built in his name.

"Just a guy, on the outside of the fence," or was he "inside, looking out"? R. E. P. hanging out in a *Hot Rod* shirt at the *Hot Rod* drag races at Riverside International Raceway in 1967. *Petersen Foundation collection*

When he sold the publishing company, the assets included five decades' worth of photographs, negatives, movie footage, and other historic materials from the PPC's archive. While the Petersen Photographic Services (PPS) archive had a full-time staff during the Petersens' ownership, it sat unmanned and unguarded for many years afterward. Materials were damaged, and some were pilfered. It was always Mr. Petersen's dream to see these invaluable materials housed at the museum, managed and protected by a full-time archivist and available for licensed use in books, and magazines. Through the considered efforts of TEN, the Petersen Automotive Museum, former PPC executive Doug Evans, SEMA, and the Petersens' generosity, this dream has become a reality. The millions of visual assets have been gathered, reorganized, digitized, and relocated to a secure haven at the Petersen Automotive Museum. It would make them happy to know that these assets are now safe and well managed.

Mr. and Mrs. Petersen, as we knew them, are gone, but they will continue to live large through the many great things they created and their many good deeds. Following its near-$100 million renovation, the Petersen Automotive Museum will remain a visible, tangible, emblematic reminder of who they were, what they did, and what they loved.

It's difficult to summarize such a big life, but we leave it to the late Carroll Shelby to drive it home with an exclamation point. He recalled to David Freiburger:

We were friends for over 50 years. I owe Pete a lot. When I introduced the Cobra, he helped promote it with articles about the car in Hot Rod and Sports Car Graphic. Every CEO in Detroit respected him. He'd tell everybody "You should see this new car Shelby's built." It's a winner.

And so were Margie and Robert E. Petersen.

OPPOSITE: It's no surprise that there would be a Hot Wheels die-cast model dedicated to Mr. Petersen. He didn't actually invent Hot Wheels, but, as a friend of the president of Mattel Toys in the 1960s, Mr. P. once observed that "you guys make all these larger car toys, but why don't you make small toys with really fast wheels and then you can sell them by the millions to kids, plus tracks, carrying cases, and all the stuff that goes with them." Sometime later, Mattel hired a team of (mostly automotive) designers to come up with a roster of models, often tricked out in bright iridescent colors; before long, Hot Wheels was born. *Author collection, Mel Stone photo*

LEFT: Even though Mr. and Mrs. P. had sold the publishing company by the time *Motor Trend* reached its fiftieth anniversary in 1999, they were always welcome to celebrate their top titles at events like this. *Author photo*

Acknowledgments

W e first acknowledge everyone who has, over time, worked at
Petersen Publishing Company, helping to deliver on the Petersens'
visions and the birth of "speed reading" in America. There are too
many to mention by name—although we will discuss a number of them
here—but everyone who played a role is important. Ditto the Petersen
Automotive Museum Directors, managers and staff, past and present.
A particular tip of the hat goes to Thomas Voehringer and Mark Han,
current managers of The Enthusiast Network Image Archive, which
granted us access to so many great photographs. We also want to
recognize public relations representatives Kahn Media, and everyone at
Quarto Publishing who supported and produced this book. A special nod
goes to Ed Iskenderian and Bruce Meyer, who authored the foreword and
one of the prefaces, along with photographers Evan Klein and Mel Stone,
and wife Linda and husband Joe. And finally, to you, dear readers, who
reached into your wallet and purchased this book: without your interest,
we'd have no reason to do this.

Thanks one and all,
Matt and Gigi

Index

....

Page locators in **bold** refer to pictures or illustrations.

About the Authors

Matt Stone former executive editor of *Motor Trend* magazine, has been a professional automotive journalist and photographer since 1985. He has authored and photographed several books, including the bestselling *365 Cars You Must Drive, My First Car, McQueen's Machines*, and *McQueen's Motorcycles*, all from Motorbooks. He lives in Glendale, California.

Gigi Carleton was lifelong friends with the Petersens. For more than forty years, she worked at Petersen Publishing Company as Margie and Robert E. Petersen's executive secretary and personal manager, having started as a temp. Following the Petersens' passing, she is now president of the Margie and Robert E. Petersen Foundation. She lives in Henderson, Nevada.